THE SPINSTER I ONCE KNEW

Based on a true story

By
Kay Marie Perrin

Copyright © 2025 by Karen Marie Perrin
ALL RIGHTS RESERVED.
No part of this book may be reproduced or transmitted by any means, electronic or mechanical, including photocopying and recording, or by any information storage and retrieval system, except as may be expressly permitted in writing from the author.
Hardcover ISBN: 978-1-965146-59-0

Dedication

This novel is dedicated to
my parents
Fred "Gus" Gustafson
and
Naoma B. Gustafson

Table of Contents

PART ONE 1

    Chapter 1 2

    Chapter 2 20

    Chapter 3 32

    Chapter 4 38

PART TWO 49

    Chapter 5 50

    Chapter 6 61

    Chapter 7 80

    Chapter 8 89

    Chapter 9 98

    Chapter 10 102

    Chapter 11 114

PART THREE 127

"Aunt Clara's Journey" 128

    Chapter 12 130

    Chapter 13 152

    Chapter 14 173

Chapter 15 194
Chapter 16 206
Chapter 17 213
Chapter 18 216
Chapter 19 221
Chapter 20 231
Chapter 21 241
Chapter 22 263
Chapter 23 274
Chapter 24 280
Chapter 25 301
Chapter 26 312
Chapter 27 332
Chapter 28 346
Chapter 29 359
Chapter 30 372
Chapter 31 390

P.S. 406

About the author 407
Discussion Questions 409

PART ONE

Chapter 1

Henry (1851) and Peter (1853) Schattinger were raised in the bustling city of Cincinnati, Ohio. As young men, they found themselves caught in the daily grind of factory life. Their hands, calloused from years of operating machines, often itched for something more adventurous. The Gold Rush of 1858-1863 had already lost much of its allure, but the idea of striking it rich in the rugged mountains of Colorado had taken hold of their dreams.

Unlike many others of their age at the time, these brothers had certain advantages. They were unburdened by the responsibilities of marriage and family, and they had managed to squirrel away a modest sum of money over the years. After long hours in the factory, they would often take on side jobs, sweat pouring down their brows, determined to escape the monotony of their daily routines. It was their diligence that allowed them to save for the journey they now contemplated. Their ultimate dream was to save enough money to purchase sufficient acreage in Colorado to become cattle ranchers. Every time they mentioned their idea, people would shake their heads and walk away. The brothers were tired of all aspects of factory work, such as the loud indoor environment, low wages, and always answering the boss. Of course, they were determined and practical but realized that purchasing a ranch would not come easy. However, they knew that staying in Cincinnati was not going to move them closer to their dream. The first step was moving to Colorado. They mapped out every detail of such a risky adventure; after all, they were city boys with only a big dream of becoming ranchers.

In 1869, the completion of the transcontinental railroad made the westward journey more accessible, and so Peter and Henry made the bold decision to leave their factory jobs behind and embark on a life-altering adventure. With their meager savings, they purchased train tickets from Cincinnati, Ohio, to the burgeoning city of Denver, Colorado.

Upon their arrival at Denver's Union Station, Peter, the younger of the two, turned to his older brother and asked, "Alright Henr, we made it. What's the plan now?"

Henry, surveying the comings and goings of the bustling station, replied, "Let's go find a bank first. With all this cash on us, I've been worried about being robbed ever since we left."

They asked one of the station workers which way to the nearest bank, then dragged their two large trunks behind them in that direction. Despite both the men and their luggage being battered by their journey, they overtook many other walkers along the dusty street, too giddy to match the pace of others. They quickly recognized the big welcoming doors of the bank as described by the station worker and were almost in an elated jog by the time they were at its doorstep. Inside the bank, Henry tended to the business of securing their finances while Peter dutifully watched over their meager belongings, his eyes soaking in the unfamiliar surroundings.

The older brother let out a sigh of relief the moment after handing over the stack of smooth, once-folded bills to the teller. Their funds were now safely deposited; the older brother returned to where his brother had remained.

"There's a diner over there," Peter said, pointing through the bank windows across the street. "A whole lot of people have gone in there while you were working on the money, so I imagine the food there can't be too bad."

Henry said he could eat and so the two slung their battered bags over their shoulders once more and headed towards the diner.

At a table beside a window, they sipped on cups of hot coffee while observing the eclectic mix of patrons. Henry's sharp eyes caught sight of a nearby table where three gentlemen, their faces still bearing the traces of their recent journey, were engaged in animated conversation.

"I'm going to ask those men over there if they know of any nearby boardinghouses," Henry declared, gesturing with one arm while rising from the table.

Meanwhile, Peter struck up a conversation with the waitress as she re-filled their cups. "Pardon me, ma'am, but would you happen to know if there are any job opportunities around here?"

The waitress shined a warm smile at Peter before responding, "New in town?"

Peter nodded.

"There's a factory located a mile south of here. Some of my husband's friends work over there, and I'm pretty sure they're always looking for new people. Men with experience in machinery, I believe." She turned her head away from the now full cups and met Peter's eyes. "Does that help you any?"

Peter nodded again, this time more vigorously, and said it most certainly helped a lot. He thanked her twice for the help, then asked if she could point him in the right direction once he'd finished his meal.

"Of course, head out the door, turn right, and walk about a mile on this here road until you reach the large brick building with the big smokestack coming out of it," she kindly instructed. "It's a modest-sized factory, but still too big to miss. Once you're there, ask for Max – he's my brother-in-law. Tell him Elizabeth sent you." And with a quick wink, she was off to the kitchen.

Henry returned to their table shortly after.

"How'd it go?" Peter asked as his brother jostled back into his seat.

"Good. I asked them if they knew about any boardinghouses nearby, and they said they're staying in one themselves right now and are pretty satisfied with the place. 'Decent conditions and reasonably priced' was how they described it."

"Where's it at?" Peter asked.

"It's about a mile up the road," Henry said.

"The waitress also mentioned that there's a nearby factory looking for workers. She said it was about a mile away, too. I know that you don't wish to return to a factory job, and neither do I, but it might point us in the right direction. After all, we have completed the first step of our plan; we are in Colorado. We can't expect too many miracles on the first day." Peter added.

Henry's face lit up a little like he'd solved a math problem he'd been working on his head for the last few minutes.

"That must be the same factory those men work. They told me the best part of the boardinghouse was the fact that it was located across from their work," Henry said.

Their first day in Denver was shaping up to be a success. After their much-needed lunch, the two brothers commemorated their good fortune with a shot of whiskey at the inviting saloon across the street. Then, the liquor even further lifting his spirits, Peter asked a stranger at the bar if he'd take a shot with the two of them to celebrate.

"On us, of course," Peter clarified. The man half-smiled at the two brothers, a bit weary of the turn of events that had interrupted his trip to the restroom, but ultimately gave in and took the tiny, sap-colored glass from Peter's outstretched hands.

"What is it we're celebrating?" the man asked, feeling obliged to make at least a little conversation before taking his leave.

The liquor had gotten to Henry, too, by this point, and he exclaimed with pride, "We arrived by train from Cincinnati a few hours ago."

"You all like Cincinnati?" the man asked politely.

"Not enough to stay!" Peter exclaimed, and the two brothers burst into laughter. The man almost got away before Henry went on.

"No, we're here to stay, and what's more, there's a factory nearby looking for workers, we hear. Well, they need men with experience working in machinery, and that's exactly what we have, so we figured we'd check it out. There's even a decent boardinghouse near the factory, too. That's something worth celebrating, isn't it?"

The man gave the two brothers each a concerned glance, for he was able to pin down exactly what factory they were referring to before Henry had even finished describing it.

"Well, boys," he said, pulling out a chair to seat himself in, "just for that drink, I'll give you a tip of advice: don't go there."

"Why not?" Peter snapped back. "The waitress we talked to thought the place was alright."

The man shook his head. "That factory pays paltry wages, and what's worse is they own the boardinghouse, too. They make money both ways: connecting you with the factory and deducting room rent and meal costs from your hard-earned wages. Sometimes, they even coerce employees into renting specialized tools for their jobs, leaving you with next to nothing. On top of all that, they lock you into a 6-month contract, ensuring you owe them money when it's over. Trust me – I worked there a little while. Yes, sir, they're a crafty bunch. You're lucky you found me."

Peter and Henry exchanged skeptical glances, questioning the trustworthiness of their newfound companion.

"What's your two boys' names, anyway?" the man asked, trying to defuse the tension if only a little.

"I'm Henry, and he's Peter," the older brother answered, "but more importantly if we can't go to that factory, what the hell else is there to do here?" Henry had built in his head a career path for the next few years from the imagined factory; this man had not done himself many favors trying to undermine it in a single swoop.

"I'm Bud," the man said. They shook hands. "Well, look here. Maybe we will have something to celebrate after all. Maybe it *is* luck you two found me here and we all shared this drink."

The brothers looked at the man like he was mad.

"I live west of Denver here in Denver, but not in the city. I actually only came into town today to hire a fellow to work on my ranch. He was supposed to meet me here in this saloon at three to discuss the matter."

The brother looked at the clock. It read half past four.

"And so, I have a proposition for you two boys. How about you both come and work on my ranch?"

"Don't you need just one worker?" Peter asked.

"I need as many as I can get!" the man laughed with a wheeze. "You two would help with tending to the horse's cattle and planting winter wheat. I'd say I pay a fair wage, and there's a cozy cabin on the property I'd let you two live in if you needed it. Wood stove, two comfortable beds, a water pump – it's nice enough to live in. I should know. I lived there myself while the main house was being built. And I'll let you both live there for, say, two dollars a month. If you keep it clean and everything else, of course."

"I'd like to see the cabin first and get a better sense of the work required," Peter said. "How many employees do you currently have?"

Henry, always the pragmatist, got right to the point, "And what's the pay like? What kind of work would we do during the winter months?"

Bud, keen to clarify the details, responded, "How about you two let me buy a round, and we'll talk it over our next drink?"

The brothers consented to this much, and Bud began to lay out his proposition as the bartender poured out their three drinks.

"I'll break it all down for you now so we won't have any misunderstandings later. Now, I've got three other ranch hands, who all live over on a property beside mine. The work is demanding, I'll admit that, and workdays are often from sunrise to sunset, six days a week. But I pay a respectable $35 a month, which includes two meals daily. I'll raise it to $40 after three months, too, if you both can prove yourselves in the field."

Bud downed his drink before adding, "And you'll gain valuable skills, too, that will serve you well if you ever dream of becoming a rancher here in Colorado. Trust me when I say those factory workers don't come close to what you can earn out in the fields."

Peter and Henry exchanged a knowing look.

"How about we accept your offer for three months at $35, and then we'll reassess after that?" Both Bud and Peter nodded in affirmation of the proposal.

Bud grinned a wide grin, extending his calloused hand, "Deal – let's shake on it."

Both brothers once again shook the man's hand, albeit this time with a level of fraternity and excitement not even the alcohol could account for.

Bud confirmed, "You 'all will need a hotel for tonight. You can stay in the same hotel where I'm staying tonight. I will meet you in the café for breakfast at 5:00 a.m. then we can pull the wagon and horses around the front for an early start. It will take most of the day to get to the ranch."

The two horses continued to pull the wagon across the vast high prairie as the sun began its descent. Bud skillfully guided his wagon under a prominent metal archway that bore the words "Golden Ranch," signaling their arrival at his property. Peter and Henry, riding in the back of the wagon, couldn't help but notice and appreciate the intricate metalwork of the sign, the craftsmanship behind it.

As they rode past the sign, they continued to soak in the breathtaking views. The sky was a light pink, which peeked through the openings of distant, white-capped mountains. They would have likely never seen something like this if they'd stayed in town at the factory, and they would've never seen anything close to it if they'd stayed in

Cincinnati. A sense of reassurance came over the pair.

With their belongings safely retrieved from the wagon, they followed Bud to the cabin, which turned out to be in surprisingly good condition. Crafted from snugly fitting logs, it featured glass windows adorned with charming calico curtains. Hooks lined the walls, providing ample space for hanging clothes, and the beds were thoughtfully furnished with springs, padding, and warm blankets. A sturdy wood stove stood in one corner, ready to provide warmth, and washbasins, pots, and pans dangled from wall hooks. A small cabinet held dishes and flatware, offering all the essentials for daily living. The place was twice as nice as where they'd lived in Cincinnati, and for a little over half the price, too.

Before leaving the two to settle into the cabin, Bud said, "Dinner is served at sundown in the dining room over at the main house. We ring the big bell about 15 minutes before sunset to make sure everyone is punctual. Be on time." Then he was gone, and the boys were finally alone together again.

Peter didn't waste a moment and immediately ventured outside the cabin to find the wood-chopping area. He was determined to start the stove, wanting a cozy cabin for the night. After quickly discovering the woodpile, he set to work, making sure to leave the stack even higher than he had found it.

By the time he returned to the cabin with an armful of firewood, Henry had already made the beds and organized their meager belongings. They used their trunks to store clothes and dry food supplies, such as black beans, dried fruit, oatmeal, and coffee. With the cabin arranged to their liking, they washed up and headed to the main house for dinner as the sun dipped below the horizon.

They knocked on the open door of the main house and were promptly welcomed by Bud, who introduced the brothers, his wife, Betty, and their children Louise, Rebecca, Charles, and Ella.

"Let's get seated so we can thank the Lord for this hot meal before it gets cold," Bud suggested.

With everyone at the table, they bowed their heads for grace. "Lord, we thank you for this food and for our new friends, Peter and Henry. Bless this family and send more rain to sprout the winter wheat. Amen," Bud prayed.

The room fell silent as everyone served themselves generous portions of the delicious home-cooked meal. Once most of the main course had been eaten, conversation broke out. Betty explained that all the children had been assigned jobs on the ranch and attended school as well. Three other ranch hands, Eddie, Tom, and Cliff, who lived on a neighboring property, had joined everyone for dinner, and we're now discussing matters of the ranch and other locals, all of which were long lost on the ignorant, happy newcomers.

For dessert, Betty served coffee and cut two impressively tasty apple pies. The children eagerly helped clear the table and wash the dishes, and Betty went to prepare a box of leftovers for Eddie, Tom, and Cliff to take back to their families.

Before Peter and Henry retired to their cozy cabin for the night, Bud offered a final reminder. "Remember to meet me at the barn at sun-up for a list of daily chores. I'll ring the big bell about 15 minutes before sunrise, so you won't miss it."

The cabin was comfortably warm by the time the two brothers returned, thanks to Peter's earlier efforts. They settled into their beds, the soft glow of a kerosene lamp providing a warm ambiance. As they drifted off to sleep, their hearts filled with gratitude for the blessings of their first day in Denver and their newfound opportunity on Bud's ranch.

The next morning, Peter and Henry were awoken by the resonant ringing of the ranch's big bell, heralding the arrival of a new day. As they groggily emerged from their warm beds, they could already hear the cheerful chatter and the clatter of utensils from the main house.

Betty, Bud's wife, had prepared a hearty breakfast featuring coffee, eggs, bacon, and toast, all of which were eagerly devoured by the field hands. The aroma of sizzling bacon and freshly brewed coffee filled the air, energizing them for the day ahead.

After breakfast, Bud outlined the day's tasks, a mixture of tending to livestock, collecting eggs from the chicken coop, and working on repairing the ranch's fences. Eddie, one of the seasoned ranch hands, was to be their guide for the day.

"Today, we're running barbed wire along the eastern fence line," Eddie directed. "The fence posts are already in place, and one wire is attached at the top. We need five wires to secure the cattle and horses. Grab some leather gloves, and we'll work until high noon."

The day unfolded about as expected for the two newcomers, with Bud making periodic appearances on horseback to inspect their progress. As the sun climbed higher in the sky, the group toiled under its warmth, securing the barbed wire to the fence posts. Bud's efficient supervision ensured that the work proceeded smoothly.

As the clock approached midday, Bud praised their efforts.

"Good work, boys. We need to have the east side of the property completely secured within a few weeks. We got to be prepared by the time September comes – Colorado winters are no joke."

Peter and Henry, their hands bearing the mark of hard work, were grateful for the opportunity to prove their worth.

After a morning of labor, Betty appeared with sack lunches for everyone.

"I've prepared these for you, Peter and Henry, as I understand you haven't had a chance to stock your cabin with food yet. It's leftovers from last night's dinner. Please help yourselves," she kindly offered.

Both brothers expressed deep gratitude for the food.

Then, with full bellies and a renewed sense of purpose, they resumed their work in the afternoon, continuing their efforts to fortify the eastern fence.

As the day waned, Peter and Henry couldn't help but feel a sense of contentment. They had arrived in Denver seeking adventure and a better life, and it seemed they had found both these things on Bud's ranch. The hard work, camaraderie, and warmth of their newfound friends had reassured them that they had made the right decision.

With the setting sun casting a golden hue over the vast Colorado landscape, the brothers knew that their journey had brought them to a place of opportunity and promise. Heading back to their cozy cabin after the long day of work, they reflected on their blessings and the adventures that lay ahead, grateful for the twists of fate that had brought them to this moment in time.

Chapter 2

Over the next eight years, Henry and Peter worked on the Golden Ranch with Bud and his crew. They were candid about their long-term goals and asked him to share his valuable knowledge. With each paycheck, they diligently squirreled away a portion, nurturing their dream of owning a ranch of their own in the future. As Bud introduced them to prominent landowners, they started asking around about available property in the area west of Denver. Bud, recognizing their ambition, granted them a few days off in spring before the onset of the winter wheat harvest.

The brothers took Bud's generous offer and made plans to investigate a section (one square mile or 640 acres) of land near Fairplay west of Denver. Bud connected them with George Williams, the owner, who was getting out of the ranching business. Before the trip, they had a long talk with Bud to get some facts about the price and if a section was sufficient for a starter ranch. Bud assured them that the deal was solid and a good place to start pursuing their dreams.

Departing from Union Station at the crack of dawn, they embarked on a journey that would shape their destiny. Their route took them through Georgetown, where they switched to a narrow-gauge train bound for Breckenridge. From there, they rented horses to traverse the 23-mile stretch to Fairplay. Arriving at the boardinghouse, they prepared for their meeting with George Williams, the proprietor of the land they were eyeing.

Over dinner, George amused them with tales of the land's history, having staked his claim to it back in 1862 during the early days of Colorado's homesteading era. As a fellow Ohioan, he shared a kinship with Henry and Peter, but it was his expertise as a rancher that truly resonated with the brothers.

George spoke, "The land is on a high prairie at about 9,200 feet, a bit down from Fairplay at 9,953. The Rockies protect the land on the west from getting deep snow, which shelters the cattle. I have been growing winter and summer wheat plus alfalfa each year. Some crops grow better than others, but I always broke even on the expenses. It fed the cattle for most years. I am selling the land for $5 per acre, which would be $3,200, but I'm willing to drop the price to an even $3000. I am sure that you have questions, so let's get the questions."

Henry asked, "What comes with the price, such as the house, barn, equipment, horses, and cattle?"

George glanced at Peter for his questions.

Peter asked, "Besides Henry's questions, when are you planning to move from the property? Also, are you willing to hold the mortgage, or will we need to get a loan from a bank?"

"Let's make this deal simple. The asking price for the land and all extras will cost you $6,000. I will hold the mortgage. The down payment is $2000, and the remainder will include the federal 5% interest rate."

Henry did some quick math and replied, "How about a pay-off of $1000 per year plus 5% interest? That would be about $90 per month total."

George seemed impressed by Henry's quick math skills because he had calculated the same deal at home before the meeting. "I think that we are close on this deal."

Peter asked, "When can we see the property tomorrow? Also, if we decide to make this deal, will you provide knowledge about the cattle, horses, and equipment? Do you have ranch hands helping with the property? If so, do they have housing?"

"Sure, I will come back tomorrow with two horses and the wagon. I will show you around the property. My wife, Elizabeth, will cook lunch. Yes, I have two hired hands, and they live in a cabin. You would make a deal with them on your own."

Henry said, "I think that we have taken enough of your time for this evening. We need to put pen to paper so we can give you an answer tomorrow.

George replied, "I will be here after breakfast, say about 8. It takes about an hour. Is that good?"

"Yes. See you in the morning. Thanks for your time."

Henry and Peter retired to their room, their minds abuzz with anticipation.

As they mulled over their conversation with George, Henry voiced his thoughts. "What are you thinking?"

Peter, ever pragmatic, suggested a cautious approach to bargaining. "Let's not reveal our hand too soon. We should haggle a bit to save some money. Remember, he homesteaded that land, so he didn't spend a dime acquiring it. Plus, we need to ensure we don't deplete our savings entirely. Emergencies can arise."

Agreeing with Peter's assessment, Henry concurred, "I agree. We can ask for a price reduction, especially since we're not insisting on a thorough inspection of the house and cabin for unforeseen damage or repairs."

With their resolve strengthened, they reaffirmed their commitment to sealing the deal the following day, eager to embark on the next chapter of their journey towards land ownership.

A year later, Henry and Peter had successfully closed the land purchase deal, acquiring an additional section on the south side of the original property. Everything fell into place seamlessly. The hired hands remained employed along with comfortable lodging in the cabin.

In matters of the heart, Henry found love in Fairplay with Joanna Place, while Peter's affections bloomed with Elizabeth Lesburg, a charming waitress from the Denver diner. The expansive ranch house accommodated both couples comfortably. Elizabeth's culinary talent provided hearty breakfasts and dinners for the brothers and their ranch hands, while Joanna undertook the responsibility of cleaning and laundry. Soon enough, the two women forged a close friendship.

Amidst the hustle and bustle of ranch life, the brothers' hard work began to yield a comfortable income. Thanks to Bud's guidance, they honed their skills, mastering the intricacies of planting and harvesting winter wheat. However, the harsh winters posed challenges for their livestock, prompting them to construct towering snow fences for protection and storage for feed. These labor-intensive efforts paid off, ensuring the survival of their cattle come spring.

In the spring of 1884, Henry and Joanna welcomed their first child, George Francis Schattinger, into the world, a joyous addition to their family. Meanwhile, Peter and Elizabeth pondered their future on the second section of land they had acquired. Peter broached the subject of purchasing the land with Henry, envisioning the construction of their own home.

"Peter," Henry responded, "That's a thoughtful proposal. Let me discuss it with Joanna, and I'll get back to you soon."

When he told Joanna, she said, "I like the idea. It is getting crowded in this house with four adults and Baby George. The only questions that I have regarding this transition are: Who is going to clean this house and do the laundry? Will I continue to be the only cook for the ranch hands and take care of George? Will the ranch hands continue to cover the work of both sections? You get those answers, then we will talk more."

Henry always realized that Joanna was a smart businesswoman. He was speechless since those practical questions had not entered his mind.

He replied sheepishly, "You are the brains in this marriage. Those are great questions. Let's talk about how to proceed with this offer."

They spent several evenings talking on the front porch while rocking little George. Joanna was convinced that Peter and Elizabeth should move, but that put a big burden on her.

Henry replied, "I could hire one or two more ranch hands so I could be home more to help with cleaning and laundry."

Joanna burst into laughter. "Henry, you have never done laundry in your life. You don't know how to scrub floors. I have the answer."

Henry leaned in and said, "What, my love, is the answer?"

Joanna replied, "You keep working with the ranch hands. It is time that I deserve to get some help with this house and the children. Also, I need new clothes if we are going to attend more community events. You make enough money to pay the guys. You can make more money to pay for my helper. How does that sound, darling?"

Henry looked stunned but said, "Joanna, as I said before, you are the brains in this house. Start looking for a suitable, correct woman to help you. And in the meantime, I will formulate a reasonable offer for Peter and Elizabeth."

Over the next year, Peter embarked on the construction of a modest house on the section of land. During this time, Peter and Elizabeth welcomed their first child, Walter, into the world. As their family grew, the brothers made the decision to divide their herd of cattle and horses. Peter managed to save enough money to hire a ranch hand to assist with the winter wheat harvest, capitalizing on the favorable weather that allowed them to accumulate substantial savings.

Meanwhile, Henry and Joanna expanded their family, welcoming two more children in the ensuing years. Grateful for her invaluable assistance, Joanna cherished the presence of Lottie, their dedicated house helper who not only excelled in cooking but also managed household chores and provided care for the children. With the addition of Mary in 1885, Henry constructed an extra bedroom adjoining the kitchen to accommodate Lottie, ensuring her comfort and convenience. Clara followed in 1887, marking the arrival of another healthy addition to their family. However, their eldest son, George, who had endured several bouts of childhood illness, required additional attention. Despite his ailments, George displayed a keen interest in learning, spending his recovery hours immersed in books and nurturing a growing fascination with science. Their youngest child, Joanna, completed their family in the latter part of the decade.

As fate would have it, the weather took a turn for the worse, subjecting the region to a prolonged drought. With no irrigation water available, the wheat crop suffered, significantly impacting the ranchers' income. The scarcity of grazing land led to the loss of most cattle herds in the Fairplay and South Park area. Fortunately, the survival of their horses, pigs, and chickens was ensured through diligent efforts to provide sufficient water.

During the drought's adversity, Peter approached Henry with a proposition that would alter the course of their lives.

He explained, "Elizabeth and I have been thinking about moving back to Denver. I have been talking to a few ranchers that have also decided to leave. The plan is to combine our talents and open a machine shop that includes welding, tool and die parts, and woodworking skills. Some kept their machine tools, just in case ranching did not work for them. One family from North Park has already left. They bought a small house with a large metal shed on the property. It is located near to the industrial area near downtown Denver."

Henry responded, "It sounds like you and Elizabeth have made a wise decision. What will you do with your section of land, including the small herd of cattle and a few horses?"

"Well, we thought that you and Joanna might be interested in a package deal. We would accept the original purchase price for the land, but now there is a small house included. Since most of the cattle were yours in the beginning, we will adjust the terms accordingly. You do not need to pay cash. A monthly payment would suit us fine while we get started in Denver."

Without any hesitation, Henry said, "Brother, you have got yourself a deal. Let's shake on it right now."

The deal was sealed.

Peter concluded, "Henry, there are several families in the area that are willing to sell their land to anyone who gives them a fair price. If you are interested, I can share their names."

"Yes, I would be interested in acquiring more land."

After Peter and Elizabeth's departure for Denver, their decision seemed to spark a trend, as several other families in the area began considering similar moves, for Henry and Joanna, this shifting landscape prompted a period of reflection and decision-making, both in terms of their family responsibilities and the taking advantage of the opportunities to expand the acreage of the ranch.

As they navigated these transitions, the relentless drought persisted, stretching beyond the initially forecasted three years and into a fourth. Without irrigation water, the challenges facing the ranchers grew ever more daunting. Financial losses mounted, and the once lush grazing land began to wither under the relentless sun.

Yet, amidst this adversity, the families of Fairplay and South Park refused to yield. Drawing upon their deep reserves of determination and ingenuity, they remained determined to overcome the obstacles and emerge stronger on the other side. Through careful management and diligent effort, they ensured that their livestock received the sustenance needed to survive by hauling water and making do with what little resources they had.

In the face of uncertainty, their collective spirit remained unbroken, a testament to the resilience and tenacity of those who called this rugged land their home.

Chapter 3

As the drought of 1897 finally released its grasp on the land, Henry Schattinger found himself eager to resume his ranching endeavors with the promise of brighter days ahead. Who would have guessed that Henry Schattinger, a factory worker in Ohio, would become a wealthy rancher in Colorado? It was true. Henry and Joanna owned under 4,500 acres of land and were firmly positioned within Fairplay's upper class. He had paid off the mortgage to Peter and other ranchers who sold him their property during the drought, which had allowed him to sustain a herd of 2800 cattle and 300 sheep. The crew he employed consisted of 20 men working the land, caring for and herding the animals, 10 men maintaining the barn, the large house, and the four houses that were scattered across the property that had been built for crew families and an additional row housing for the single men. A true sign of his wealth was the luxury of indoor plumbing and electric lights. Even at Fairplay's City Hall, government officials and other bureaucrats shared the luxury of indoor plumbing with two indoor toilets for the three floors worth of workers employed there, distributed on opposite sides of the building; at Schattinger's house, the two bathrooms of the house were separated by nothing more than a brief walk down the hall.

One evening, the family gathered around the warmth of the hearth for a lively conversation.

"Do you think the grass will grow higher and greener this year?" asked young George, who had never seen in all his short life since Fairplay was withered and dry as it had been over the past few years.

"I sure hope so," replied Henry with a reassuring smile. "With the rain returning, I think the pastures will start looking green again soon."

Mary, Henry's thoughtful oldest daughter, said, "I'm glad for the rain. We won't need to haul water for the animals as much now."

"Did you ever think we'd see the ranch green after the drought?" Clara interjected. "I thought a lot more of the animals were gonna die before the drought ended. I thought enough of them might have died that we would've had to move to the city and live there for a while until the rain came back.

Henry's gaze softened. "Well, Clara, there were times when I wasn't so sure it would all work out either. But with hard work and a bit of luck, we have reached the other side of the drought, I hope."

Across the room, Joanna spoke up.

"Speaking of luck, George, your birthday is fast approaching. I remember when you were a young child, your dad and I prayed every night that you would live another day. You were so sick – I can remember how faint your breathing was back then, how much you'd burn up under all those blankets like it was yesterday. Sometimes, I really thought you weren't going to make it. And now here we are, celebrating your 14th birthday, bless the Lord." She wiped away a single tear that had found its way out. "Have you given any thought to how you'd like to celebrate?"

George's face lit up with excitement. "Well, Ma, I've been thinking about that a bit, and I've decided I'd like to go with Pa to Silverthorne and visit a silver mine over there. The ranch crew says the mines are quite a sight, and I've been reading up on metallurgy and mining for a few months now, too."

"A fine idea, George," Henry said, nodding approvingly. "A bit of adventure to mark your fourteenth year. Maybe you can even teach me a thing or two about the mines while we're there since you've been reading up on it all so much. I'm sure it will be great to make the trip. We will stay over one night to give the horses a good rest."

With plans for George's birthday set in motion, the family turned their attention to their ongoing commitment to community service.

Mary and Clara, co-chair of the town's thrift store, had seen lots of needy families come by the store as of late and were hoping her family could help her come up with some ideas as to how the store could help these people in need. Mary was the organizer of the thrift store, but Clara was the person who always thought of new ideas. She wanted to try new ideas, such as having sales.

Mary would retort by saying, "Clara, it is a thrift shop. We don't have sales because all the items are used and cheap."

Clara replied, "But the clothing racks are full because no one is buying used clothing. I want to try a sale where all clothing items are priced at 10 cents for the first week of every month. Then we could change the sale to something like the second week of every month; all leather shoes are 25 cents. The sale will catch on, and the community, not just those in need, will stop by to browse through the sale items."

Mary scoffed, "Well, your idea is better than what we are doing now that is not working."

"Pa, do you think there's anything we could donate to the thrift store? There're several families that have recently moved here to Fairplay, and I think we ought to help them get started setting up if there's anything we can do for them."

"What if we donate some of my old baby clothes?" inquired Joanna, her youthful voice filled with eagerness.

Their mother pondered it all over for a moment before replying, "Well, I guess we won't need those clothes anymore, will we? If you think another family could use them, Joanna, you're welcome to take them."

"If you're planning on bringing a lot of things to the store, put your donations in the kitchen by tomorrow morning before chores, Joanna. I'm taking the wagon into town to get supplies tomorrow, so I can drop off the donations if you need them."

Then Clara looked at Mary and asked, "Are you available this afternoon to help me make the signs for advertising the thrift store sale? Monday is the first week of the month, so the timing is perfect. I will spread the word around the four other thrift store volunteers while I am in town."

Mary sneered, "Sure. Now that it looks like you are taking charge of the thrift store."

Henry cleared his throat after this and began speaking again, but this time in a firmer and commanding tone.

"Remember, children; we'll be attending the community dinner this Sunday. The Mason Lodge is awarding us the Outstanding Citizens' Award for our contributions to Fairplay, and I expect each and every one of you to be well-dressed and on your best behavior."

Chapter 4

By 1903, 16-year-old Clara was finishing high school in Fairplay, Colorado, while her older brother, George, was studying engineering at Colorado State University. Clara felt restless and uninspired by high school, craving adventure and new experiences.

She wanted to gain some insight into college, so she asked George, "What is college like? Am I going to be bored like I am in high school?"

"Clara, if you expect to enjoy college, you must change your attitude. You always think that you are above everyone else. Sorry, sister, but you are the same as most people."

Clara walked away and, over her shoulder, said, "I will prove you wrong."

Unsure of her true passion, she decided to enroll in the Teacher's College for Women in Greeley, Colorado. She chose this predominantly female institution to avoid the distraction of men seeking wives, focusing instead on her goal of meeting interesting people and graduating quickly.

The teacher certificate program was a two-year degree that Clara aspired to complete swiftly, then sought employment in a vibrant city filled with art, music, and bookstores.

Her parents drove her to the bus station in Fairplay.

Her father gave her a hug and pushed a roll of cash into her palm as he said, "Take care and enjoy college. Drop us a note when you have time."

Her mother gave her a bit of typical advice by saying, "Never leave without lipstick and a smile."

Clara waved goodbye as she boarded the bus to Greeley, Colorado. Upon arrival, she took a taxi to her assigned women's dormitory. Clara found her roommates, who were around her age, to be dull and immature. She remembered her brother's advice, so before the end of the first week, she registered for art and music courses in addition to her education classes to enrich her experience.

She thought to herself, "Well, George was finally right for the first time."

Through her electives, she made a few friends who shared her interests. Together, they frequently took the bus to Denver on weekends to attend concerts and visit art museums.

Clara quickly realized she loved city life. Despite her father's successful ranching career, Clara knew a lifestyle surrounded by animals and dirt was not to her liking. She dreamed of a future in a bustling city, far from the quiet ranch life where she grew up.

Clara, an intelligent and dedicated student, completed the two-year program at the Teacher's College for Women by May 1905. She moved to Denver, quickly finding a boardinghouse run by Mrs. Wilson, and settled into a room overlooking the city park. Determined not to settle for a boring job and funded by her parents, Clara spent the summer searching for a teaching position that suited her interests. She was particularly intrigued by the Montessori method, which she had studied in college.

Clara found a match at the Opportunity School, run by Miss Emily Griffith, who believed in providing education for everyone. After an enthusiastic interview, Clara was offered the job.

Mrs. Griffith said, "Let's go on a tour so you can see and meet some of the other teachers. There are a few here today. School does not start for two weeks but they are preparing their classrooms."

As Clara was looking at her classroom, Mrs. Griffith handed Clara a large envelope and said, "In that envelope, you will find a list of the nine children in your class. Also, there is a sheet for each student with the name, age, school last attended, and parents' names. After you review the information, you should keep that envelope locked in your desk and here is the key to your desk."

Clara enjoyed meeting the other teachers. They were welcoming and willing to provide Clara with a few tips, such as where to purchase art supplies to decorate her classroom or where the coffee was in the teachers' lounge. By the end of the tour, Clara thanked Mrs. Griffith for the opportunity to get started on this new adventure as a grade schoolteacher.

She walked to the art supply store a few blocks from the school. As expected, she left with several heavy bags of supplies and decided to take the bus back to her boardinghouse.

With giddy excitement, Clara played with the ample supplies on her bedspread; then, she located her "The Montessori Method" textbook. As she thumbed through her textbook, she recalled the 4 C's of Montessori Principles: critical thinking, collaboration, creativity, and communication.

The rest of the afternoon, she scanned the information in the envelope. As she read the detailed description of each child, she found ways to connect their name to their life story. Clara thought that she had found her life's passion sitting on her bed that afternoon.

The following two weeks, she was in her classroom decorating the bulletin boards, making lesson plans, making friends, and receiving valuable advice from seasoned teachers.

On the first day of school, Clara quickly fell in love with her students and began creating custom activities for each child. Despite never wanting children of her own, the students brought her joy each day. Her innovative lesson plans impressed Mrs. Griffith, and parents adjusted to the creative, engaging homework assignments. Clara's dedication and passion for teaching transformed her classroom while making her a beloved teacher at the Opportunity School.

Clara sustained her love of teaching at the Opportunity School for eight years. By 1910, she had formed friendships in Denver and was ready to move out of the boardinghouse. Her parents retired and relocated to Denver, purchasing a two-story home on Lincoln Ave near the State Capitol.

The Spinster I Once Knew | 43

Clara moved in with them while continuing to teach.

During weekends, Clara began involving herself in local politics, finding it a refreshing diversion from teaching. She participated in campaign activities for State Senator John B. Stephen, the Republican candidate who lost to Democrat Governor John Shafroth in 1910. Clara, then 23, attended fundraising events and frequently dined with Stephen, sparking rumors about their relationship, though it eventually faded.

Clara's parents became prominent in Denver society by joining the Denver Country Club and participating in elite circles. Her father reestablished his leadership in the Masonic Temple, and her mother focused on founding the Denver Art Museum and maintaining a high-class wardrobe. Concerned about Clara remaining unmarried, they encouraged her to attend high-society events. Despite her stunning beauty, wardrobe, and class, Clara disliked the small talk and gossip. Some viewed her as merely an elementary school teacher, not a suitable match for their sons, but Clara was unaffected by the snobbish remarks, focusing instead on her goal of traveling the world on her terms.

Then, one afternoon after school, her mother mentioned, "Clara, there is a fund-raising event at the Denver Library. Your father and I purchased tickets, but we have a Mason Lodge event. I think it would be good if you could represent us at the library tonight so we can use at least one of the two tickets."

Clara yawned, "I will go since I can walk down to the library from here. It will be nice to get outside. When does it start?"

"Can you show the smallest part of enthusiasm at the event? You do love the library. I think you should wear your blue wool dress with that lovely silk scarf with the embroidery details."

"I am old enough to select my own outfit, Mother."

"Yes, you are old enough, but I have a better sense of fashion. Don't forget to take lipstick for a touchup," reinforced her mother.

Clara defiantly wore the recommended blue wool dress to avoid another conversation with her mother as she walked out the door.

Much to her surprise, while standing in line for a glass of wine, she met a gentleman named Captain Greg Williams. Much to her surprise, she found him to be interesting.

Before the evening was over, Clara asked, "What kind of a captain are you?"

Greg shared a bit of his story in his response, "The short answer is my parents owned a large import business in New York City, so we traveled a lot in my childhood. I got interested in sailing while I attended Harvard. After my parents retired, I continued the family business after purchasing a yacht. I am the captain."

Clara found him to be intriguing. After talking for most of the evening, they exchanged contact information before departing. While walking home, Clara glanced at his card and realized that he lived a few blocks from her parents.

Much to her surprise, Greg called her the following evening. They agreed on a date and time for dinner. Since her mother was in the room and heard the conversation, she questioned Clara after the call.

"Who is he? Did you meet him at the library event? I told you that you needed to get out more. What is his name? Where did he go to college?"

"Stop, Mother. His name is Captain Greg Williams. He graduated from Harvard and inherited an import business from his parents. He owns a yacht. That is enough for now."

Her father was in the room listening and added, "I know Greg Williams. His wife passed away a few years ago. I think he has a few children."

"Perfect. Clara, you could get married and have an instant family. What a great package deal," stated her mother with sarcasm.

At that point, Clara left the room for some peace and quiet.

After dining together several times, Greg asked, "How would you like to go for a walk after dinner this evening? The weather is so nice."

Clara replied, "That would be lovely."

"Thanks. I would like to share some of my life story with you."

"Of course," Clara said.

"I think that I mentioned that my wife passed away from cancer several years ago."

Clara nodded as they strolled down the well-lit promenade of 16th Street.

"Well, I have not mentioned that I have seven children," stated Greg, and then he paused to get Clara's response.

"What are their ages?" said Clara casually.

"They range from 4 years old to 19 years old. Three boys and four girls. Currently, they live with their maternal grandparents in Los Angeles while I complete some business in Denver. They are great and fun children. I miss them each day."

Clara nodded.

Greg stopped and turned to sit on a park bench. He ushered Clara to sit next to him, and then he leaned in and said, "May I ask you a question?" Clara nodded. She gasped silently while thinking that he was about to propose to her.

"I would like to ask you if you would consider homeschooling my children on the yacht during our next Pacific voyage for my import business. I will offer a generous salary, including a private suite. I have a chef and maid, so teaching will be your only responsibility. We won't leave for a few months so that you can complete the semester at your current job. Since the children are in California, you will not meet them prior to the voyage."

Clara nodded.

"I will let you think about this proposition for a week before you give me your final answer."

PART TWO

Chapter 5

As a young child, I couldn't shake the feeling that there was something peculiar about Aunt Clara's house. Her brick house was built in 1918 in downtown Denver, a few blocks from the Capital Building of Colorado. Despite having visited numerous times, her house stood as a puzzle in my young mind, and it never failed to give me an eerie feeling.

On a winter Sunday afternoon, my parents made the decision to pay Aunt Clara a visit. Since she never married or had children, my father felt a sense of obligation to visit periodically as her nephew. Also, her house was four blocks away from my paternal grandmother Joanna's residence in downtown Denver. This proximity allowed my parents to visit both elderly women on the same day.

"How old is Aunt Clara?" I asked in the car to break up the long drive.

"She was born in 1887, so use your new math skills to figure out her age," my dad responded.

The Spinster I Once Knew | 51

"I was born in 1953, so she was 66 when I was born. I'm seven, so seven plus 66 makes her 73."

Dad nodded in the rearview mirror as he pulled into a parking place near her house. Since it was snowing, our footprints marked the sidewalk.

I noticed the same thing creepy characteristics each visit as I thought to myself, "Aunt Clara's front porch spanned the width of the house. The top half of the front door had four windowpanes, and the bottom half was wood in dire need of fresh paint. The two rusty mailboxes attached to the brick next to the door frame."

Dad said, "I will knock on the door. It will take a long time, but we will eventually hear her unhurried footsteps."

I had memorized the sound of her walk because it was immediately identifiable by the old black oxford shoes with stacked heels she always wore. She was a tall, slender woman with shoulder-length white-blond hair and a face that was perpetually stern.

When the door swung open, I could see her hair on her shoulders. I was pleased with my memory, I thought, "Yes, I am right again."

I always felt a sense of unease whenever she opened the door.

She said, "I was not expecting you."

I thought again, "How could she ever expect us? Since she didn't own a telephone, we had no way to communicate before our visits. This situation added an element of uncertainty to our impromptu visits."

I recognized the next step by thinking, "Once her impression of surprise faded, next came an air of anger and frustration, as though we were interrupting some vague, undisclosed plans of hers. The only thing that changed was she must have noticed that it was snowing, because she laid down an old, frayed rug for us to wipe off our wet shoes."

No matter how many times we visited, she would explicitly warn us by saying, "Stay away from those stairs. Three single businessmen live up there."

In my memory, I heard my dad say, "Not one person in the family had ever caught a glimpse of these supposed tenants."

We proceeded down the long hallway straight ahead leading to a closed door on the right. Aunt Clara lived behind the closed door.

I had this place memorized. I thought, "The door on the right at the end of the long hallway opened into a shabby dining room, where a single light bulb dangling from the plaster ceiling illuminated the large oval dark wood table and the four well-worn padded chairs tucked beneath it. At any given time, she had one light on. Never more than one light, never less than one."

Once I asked her about the light, she replied, "I see no point in wasting electricity. You should live the same way."

Sometimes, she followed up this comment with another of her favorite phrases, "You go sit on the black trunk without objection."

Dad obliged her by boosting me onto the trunk.

To occupy myself, I thought about what it was Aunt Clara stashed in the truck beneath me. I never tried to find out what was in there.

Mom always reminded me, "Do not touch anything in her house. She gets mad easily."

After neutralizing me, Aunt Clara motioned to my parents, "Sit at the dining room table."

They obeyed, sitting opposite each other, while Aunt Clara always sat at the head of the table. Also seated at the table were stacks of newspaper clippings, unopened mail, her portable typewriter, and a small radio.

An avid fan of professional baseball, she listened to all her baseball games on that radio. She would also use it to listen to the radio show hosted by famous American Christian televangelist Oral Roberts, co-founder of Oral Roberts University.

As I did not pay attention to the conversation with Aunt Clara rather I scanned two tall wooden bookshelves covered in dust and loaded with her favorite books. I was never able to make out the title of the books. I thought to myself, "If I could see the letters, it would not help. I was just starting to learn to read."

After I got bored with the bookshelves, I turned to my right to peer into the sitting room that faced the street. I liked the high ceiling archway that divided the rooms. The large window had multiple panes covered with soiled, sheer yellow drapes, but I watched blurry snowflakes fall in the streetlights. The furniture in that small room consisted of a dusty red velvet loveseat, two wooden side tables, an upholstered needlepoint footstool, and a single Tiffany glass reading lamp. I noticed the frayed cloth-covered cord of the reading lamp looked like a fire hazard.

I remember that on our last visit, Dad asked, "Clara, would you like for me to change the cord on that lamp the next time we come to visit?"

"If I wanted the cord changed, I would have changed it myself, so no."

When I looked left past the dining room table, I practiced thinking about what I committed to memory on the last visit. My mind raced, "The corner was what Aunt Clara referred to as her bedroom. There were no walls separating the dining room from her bedroom. The area was dark, but I could see a single metal bed with a thin mattress. It was topped with a pile of old-fashioned quilted blankets but no sheets or pillows. Besides the bed was a wooden nightstand on which a small table light rested, though it was evident that the light was not in use for as long as I had been visiting, for I never saw a lightbulb in it."

I looked closer and thought, "The nightstand also had three drawers, the middle drawer of which was missing its knob" I had not noticed those details previously.

I continued to put more details in my brain, "Off to the side, a hook held her nightgown and tattered woolen robe. A makeshift closet, with two rods drilled into the plaster wall, displayed several dresses, blouses, skirts, and a winter coat. Below the hanging rods was a small leather suitcase sitting on its side to serve as a shoe rack for three pairs of shoes, two winter hats, and two old leather purses."

I will never forget this memory, "There was a large, dirty, threadbare Oriental rug next to her bed. Once, she told me that she bought that rug in China but never added any details."

She said, "I practice yoga daily on that rug before walking to the grocery store."

The rest of the space was firmly locked in my mind, "Straight ahead, there was a single, white door dividing the kitchen from the one large room. Aunt Clara used a small bronze horse door stop to keep the white door slightly ajar. I was never allowed to enter the kitchen, but I could always see a narrow slice of it, nonetheless. The kitchen had white shelving and a farm-style sink with a few cabinets across the bottom. The linoleum floor was black, gray, and white; it needed vigorous scrubbing. Thick dirt!"

On top of not possessing a television and telephone, Aunt Clara's house did not have a refrigerator or a stove, either. Instead, she relied on a two-burner hotplate and her electric tea kettle. On open shelves, she displayed her limited collection of dishes, bowls, and pots.

She said, "I take pride in abstaining from sugar and dairy products. They lack valuable nutrition. A complete waste of money. I walk to the grocery store daily to buy fresh meat, fruit, and vegetables."

Once, she told me, "I save the fruit and vegetable seeds for planting, evidenced by the little clay pots on my kitchen windowsill."

I never noticed if there were ever any fruits from her gardening efforts.

As for her bathroom, I have no description. Since I was barred from access to the kitchen, I assumed that it was necessary to go through the kitchen to reach her bathroom.

Chapter 5

After about an hour of sitting on the trunk, I began to sense it was almost time to leave. I had witnessed this ending many times. Aunt Clara had begun to start an argument. Though I did not understand the topic of the quarrel, I knew how it would end.

Dad said, "Yes, I understand your point."

Mom said, "It's getting late, and the roads will be slick soon. We need to get home. Kay has school tomorrow."

Aunt Clara replied stiffly, "Yes, it would be best if you left my house now."

I jumped off the trunk with glee. Mom grabbed the coats; Dad opened the door.

Over his shoulder, he said, "We'll be back in a few weeks."

Again, on the ride home, I asked a question, "Have you seen Aunt Clara's bathroom?"

"It has a small shower and toilet with only one single-bulb ceiling light and a hand-held mirror hanging on a hook over the pedestal sink," Mom replied with exhaustion.

As an inquisitive 6-year-old child, one question always follows the last question. "Well, how does she wash her clothes?"

Mom answered dryly. "Probably in the kitchen sink, but I don't know for sure, and it really does not matter. Please, no more questions."

I stopped asking questions, but I did not stop thinking about Aunt Clara's mysterious nature and peculiar actions that always intrigued me. On this ride home, I thought about how the two sisters lived four blocks away; they rarely visited each other. I couldn't help but feel there was an underlying mystery surrounding Clara's behavior.

I thought about the time when my grandmother described one incident by telling me, "Clara walked over to my house to borrow a few postage stamps. However, on one occasion, I got frustrated when Clara failed to replace the stamps even after six months had passed. So, I decided to stop speaking to Clara for three years."

Throughout my life, I was left wondering about the underlying reasons for her distant behavior and the mysterious nature of her actions. Perhaps there were deeper personal or family issues that I was unaware of, or perhaps she simply had her own idiosyncrasies and reasons for keeping her distance. The enigma surrounding her house remained a constant source of curiosity and speculation for me.

As a 6-year-old child, my perception of my great aunt was influenced by the mysterious aura surrounding her. The unusual nature of the house, coupled with the intermittent visits and the absence of modern communication methods, only added to the sense of intrigue and the feeling that there was more to Aunt Clara's world than met the eye.

Chapter 6

One year, my parents decided to have Grandma Joanna and Aunt Clara over for Thanksgiving dinner. However, they agreed that the dinner invitation would be the Saturday after Thanksgiving, so as not to miss dinner at my maternal grandparents, Grandpa and Grandma's Hursting's house.

Dad said, "Hello, Mom, how are you doing today?"

Grandma Joanna replied, "How do you think I am? I am expecting my next piano student, so make it quick."

"Naoma and I would like to invite you and Clara over for dinner on Saturday, November 24th. We will pick you and Clara up around 2:00 p.m. We will take you home around 5:00 p.m. Would you ask Clara and let me know?"

Grandma's voice was loud when she said, "Ok, I will ask her, but I doubt she will come. Is this a post-Thanksgiving dinner? What are you doing on Thanksgiving Day? I suspect you will be celebrating elsewhere, and we are an afterthought, right?"

Dad said, "You and Clara are invited to come over for dinner. Let us know if you wish to accept the invitation."

Dad sighed as Mom got dinner on the table.

I asked, "Are you going to cook a Thanksgiving dinner?"

Mom said, "Yes, it is an easy meal to prepare. If they decide not to come, then we will have delicious leftovers. How does that sound?"

Dad and I both agreed with Mom's plan.

As the day approached, Mom started preparing for dinner. Since she made a few food items for Grandpa and Grandma's dinner, such as the dinner rolls and a relish tray, she made two. One for Thanksgiving Day and one for Saturday. Mom worked full-time, but she got Friday after Thanksgiving off. I did not have to go to school, so we worked together to clean the house and get the dining room table set, including polishing the silver flatware.

On Friday evening, Granda Joanna called. I answered the phone, but when I heard her voice, I handed the phone to Mom.

Grandma said, "Hello, Naoma. I want to let you know that Fred can pick up Clara and me tomorrow around 1:00 p.m. instead of 2:00 p.m., as Fred suggested. We want to be home before dark. Please pick me up first, so I can sit in front of your car. We can drive to Clara's. She will sit in the back seat. Remember that we do not cook, so do not expect us to bring any food for dinner."

Mom, with tensed lips, she replied, "That will be fine. We are looking forward to seeing you and Clara tomorrow."

After mom hung up the phone, I mumbled, "Well-played, Mom." She smiled and made a mental note to tell Dad about the change in the pick-up time.

On Saturday morning, Mom made a hearty breakfast for everyone because she anticipated that the day might be stressful. I loved having scrambled eggs and toast on Saturday because I ate oatmeal on school days.

Chapter 6

Mom always said, "Oatmeal will stick to your ribs and give you the energy to learn throughout the school day."

After breakfast, Mom started preparing the stuffing for the turkey and peeling the potatoes. The dinner rolls, relish tray, and cranberries were prepared on Thursday, so I helped by washing the breakfast dishes and staying out of her way.

I asked, "I think that the table needs a centerpiece decoration. Can I work on it?"

Mom nodded, and I got to work. I collected two crystal candleholders, a vase, a lace placemat, and two new tapered green candles in the top drawer of the buffet. Since the good porcelain dishes had small border green leaves around the gold edge, the green candles matched. I went outside to Mom's herb garden and cut a bouquet of mint, lemon sage, and a hint of lavender. I worked quietly in the dining room so I could surprise Mom with the table decoration. I spent the next twenty minutes folding the freshly ironed napkins for each place setting.

I called, "Mom, is this how you want the napkins folded?" I wanted to get her to peek around the kitchen doorway to see my accomplishments.

She glanced at the table and, with a big smile, said, "You have made my day. The table looks beautiful, and the herbs will cleanse any negative energy during dinner."

I knew exactly what she meant without another word.

After Dad finished fixing the leg on a dining room chair, he took a quick shower and got ready to pick up Grandma Joanna and Aunt Clara.

I said, "Hey, Dad, do you want me to go with you to pick them up?"

He said, "That would be great. You can provide some funny stories and jokes to entertain them in the car."

With the fun response, I ran to my bedroom to change out of my jeans and into a dress, fancy lace-trimmed socks, and my Sunday church shoes.

The ride to Grandma Joanna's was entertaining. Dad loves country music, so he sings along with every song on his favorite radio station. He always makes car rides educational by teaching me directions and street names. His hope was that if I learned early, I wouldn't get lost when I got my driver's license. Denver is easy to learn because the Rocky Mountains are always in the west.

If there was enough time, Dad would tell me to give him directions to Grandma's house. After many of my failed attempts when he needed to take over the directions, I got reasonably well at directing Dad to her house. Since we frequently visited Aunt Clara before or after Grandma, I learned the directions to both houses. It was easier to walk to each house than drive because most streets downtown were one-way.

Back to the story, Dad and I arrived at Grandma's house at 12:55 p.m. On time for her 1:00 p.m. pickup request. Dad parallel-parked on the street. As we walked up the sidewalk to her front porch, we heard piano music. This meant only one thing: she was still teaching her piano student last Saturday morning. Grandma had strict rules for us about never interrupting her lessons.

Since we did not know when the piano lesson started, we had no idea how long we would wait. It was chilly, so we walked back to the car. We sat in the car and talked. Occasionally, I rolled down the passenger window to check if the piano lesson ended.

Finally, the piano music stopped.

Dad sighed as he looked at his watch and said, "Wait until the student comes out of the door."

The student came out and was greeted by a female adult who must have been waiting in a nearby parked car.

We walked up the sidewalk and onto the porch for a second time. Dad knocked, but Grandma did not answer. He said, "Perhaps she is in the bathroom." He knocked again.

Grandma opened the door and said, "Why are you here so early? I told you that I taught until 1:30. Come in and sit down while I change my dress."

We sat on the couch and waited. We knew that she said, "Pick us up at 1:00 p.m."

After a few minutes, she reappeared in a different dress and the same old lady's black leather oxford shoes that tie. She had her purse in hand and reached for her coat.

She said, "I am ready, and the two of you are still sitting on the couch. Let's go. Clara is waiting."

Chapter 6

We walked to the car, and Dad opened the front door for his mom. I got in the backseat.

Dad drove silently to Aunt Clara's house. He relaxed because his mother was not talking. Thankfully there was an open parking place on the street in front of Aunt Clara's house.

Dad asked, "Mom, do you want to come with me to get Clara, or do you wish to stay in the car with Kay?"

I silently crossed my fingers, but today was not my lucky day.

Grandma said, "I will wait in the car. There is no need for me to see Clara's house. I know what it looks like."

Dad walked to the front porch. As Grandma dozed off after a busy morning of teaching children piano lessons, I sighed and thought, "Great, no need for conversation."

Dad held Aunt Clara's elbow as she inched her way down the four front steps. There was a metal railing, but she was not using it. I thought, "She is a stubborn old woman."

As they approached the car, I jumped out to open the back door. Grandma was asleep in the front seat. Aunt Clara has little experience getting in and out of cars, so she awkwardly folded in half and wedged herself into the back seat. I shut the door after noting that all body parts were out of the way.

As Dad started the engine, he gave me a quick smile, and we were off. The radio was on at a low volume. Both old ladies refused to wear hearing aids, so it was fine to have the radio on. Grandma woke up and was somewhat startled by seeing her sister, Clara. They exchanged a few words while Dad and I remained silent for the remainder of the ride.

We arrived home about an hour later than expected, but Mom had that calculated before we left the house. She had time for a shower and a cup of tea and was wearing her pretty floral-patterned dress. We went through the back door because it was attached to the garage and only had one step. Dad helped Grandma out of the car and then handed her off to Mom to help her up the steps. The process was repeated for Aunt Clara.

They had been to our house numerous times, so they knew how to walk through the kitchen to get to the living room.

Following a little small talk, Mom said, "Would you each like a small glass of your favorite sherry wine?"

Grandma and Aunt Clara replied, "Yes, that would be good."

My 4-year-old sheltie collie dog, Tippy, entertained the ladies by dropping his ball at their feet. Grandma had nothing to do with Tippy, but Aunt Clara tossed his ball. Besides the sherry, the ladies enjoyed the pre-dinner conversation with me.

I asked, "What was school like when you were kids?" and "Did you have a dog when you were growing up?" While they were telling me stories, Dad excused himself to carve the turkey while Mom arranged the serving dishes on the table.

Since my topics were not controversial, they shared some stories that used up time until Mom had dinner on the table. As I filled the water glasses, Dad helped Grandma and Aunt Clara to the table. They sat on one side of the table, I sat on the opposite side, Dad sat at the head, and Mom was at the end closest to the kitchen.

I asked, "Mom, is it time to light the green candles?"

Mom replied by handing me a book of matches.

When everyone was comfortable in their chair, Dad said, "Bless this food and the family around this table with us today. Amen."

I noticed that Dad omitted the Catholic blessing that we recited as a family at every meal. This choice decreased any chance of lighting a religious fuse with his mom between the Lutherans and the Catholics.

I thought, "Good choice, Dad. You saved dinner today."

Mom stood and took the serving dishes one-by-one, so the ladies were able to scoop out their portion from each bowl. The meal was simple, with the traditional turkey, stuffing, mashed potatoes, gravy, green beans, cranberry sauce, and homemade biscuits with butter. Both ladies had full sets of dentures, so Mom kept the food choice soft, easy to eat, and tasty.

Aunt Clara reminded us by saying, "I still walk every day to the grocery store a few blocks from my house. Does anyone else bother to get fresh food every day to maintain the highest nutrients?"

Chapter 6

Silence fell over the dinner table.

Aunt Clara said, "When I traveled to India, the working women started the lentil soup in the morning, then they would go to the open market to get fresh vegetables on their way home. I can't see why working women cannot do the same thing." She paused, and no one commented.

She tried again by saying, "Doesn't anyone care about healthy food? If not, you will all die at an early age."

Her sister, Joanna, said, "Is that the only thing that you ever talk about? Why not tell Kay a story about your world travels and the children that you taught?"

I had one thought, "I don't want to hear about her world travels."

I felt a nudge under the table from Dad's foot. I said, "Yes, please tell me about the seven children that you homeschooled on the yacht. How did you manage to teach seven children when each child was in a different grade level."

My mom had heard the stories many times, so she excused herself to go start the coffee. Lucky mom, she had an escape route, and I was trapped at the table.

I thought, "We have almost averted an argument. Let's see if I continue the calm trend by asking about their childhood."

I proceeded, "Tell me what it was like to live on the cattle ranch in South Park."

I knew better than to ask about their two older siblings. No one knew why Joanna and Clara never associated with George and Mary. All four siblings lived in the metropolitan area of Denver for their entire life.

Since I was on a positive roll with questions, I asked Aunt Clara to tell me how she had the opportunity to travel so much.

This time, she started with a little background, so I was interested.

"As I child, I always wanted to find a way to escape the dreadful life on the ranch. After high school, I went to college at Colorado Teacher's College in Greeley. I have no idea why I did that because I never liked children. I taught at Montessori School in Denver for several years. All I ever wanted to do was travel the world. So, at age 32, I attended an event at the Denver Library where I met Captain Greg Williams. We became friends. He was recently widowed and needed help with the children. He owned an import business and lived on a yacht. He offered me a job to homeschool his children on his yacht. I said yes instantly. It was my dream come true! I finished the semester at the Montessori School, packed my belongings in a trunk and several pieces of luggage, got a passport, and set sail out of Los Angelos with his seven children. Our first stop was Hawaii. I was so excited!"

Just as the conversation was getting interesting, Grandma, Clara's younger sister, interrupted the conversation. "I went to Julliard in New York City for four years, and no one made a fuss about my travels. Clara got all the attention."

And so, the bickering began. Dad smiled at me to say that this was not my fault.

The sisters squabbled about their younger years for a few minutes. Fortunately, they were unable to remember many of the details, and their energy diminished rather quickly.

At that point, Mom had the pumpkin, apple, and mincemeat pies on the table, ready to be served.

She poured the coffee first. Clara asked for black coffee with a slice of pumpkin pie and Grandma asked for sugar with a slice of apple pie.

I thought, "That figures. Those two sisters had always been as different as night and day."

The conversation changed to the forecasted snowstorm heading towards Denver in the next few days.

Dad said, "Kay, did you see on the news that a big snowstorm was headed for the Rockies? That means you will be skiing early this year."

"I was hoping to get my skis out over the weekend, so you might be able to check the bindings and help me to get them waxed for the early wet snow."

Clara added, "We had cross-country skis when we were kids on the ranch. It was always cold and windy, but we had fun."

Grandma mumbled, "It was always freezing, and we had to share the skis. It was miserable for months."

Since the sun was low in the sky, so Dad said, "That was a fabulous dinner and dessert, but I think it is about time to get these ladies back home before it gets too late."

Since we had plenty of leftovers earlier in the week, Mom packed a leftover box for each of the ladies. She had been saving small containers and jars for this exact reason. Aunt Clara was especially impressed with the package of recycled containers. They appreciated the thoughtfulness of having at least two meals of leftovers.

I thought, "I doubt Clara will eat the leftovers. She does not own a refrigerator and insists on purchasing fresh food each day. However, for once, she was acting slightly cordial."

It took Mom a few seconds to get their coats off the bed in my parents' room.

She said, "I will ride with you since I have been standing in the kitchen all day."

I wanted to scream, "Then I will have to be sandwiched between the old ladies for an hour."

However, I kept quiet, knowing that I would have the backseat to myself on the way back home, and besides, Mom deserves some rest.

The drive was pleasant and silent. Both ladies were content holding their bag of leftovers on their lap. We dropped off Aunt Clara first. Dad helped her back up the front porch stairs and down the hallway to her front door. I went with him to stretch my legs from being in the backseat.

She said, "Here, take my keys. You can unlock the door and turn on the one-hanging light bulb over the dining table. Leave the bag of food on the table."

As we left, I wondered what she did with the food perhaps she ate it before she went to bed.

The next stop was Grandma's house. Dad and I repeated the same procedure.

Grandma said, "Leave the food on the piano bench. I will put it in the refrigerator after you leave."

On the way home, I thought, "I have never once been offered any type of food at Grandma Joanna's house, not even Halloween or Christmas candy. Nothing. That behavior is weird for any grandparent."

I did not know if she had enough money. She never talked about shopping or getting anything new.

I asked, "Does Grandma enjoy teaching piano lessons to children, or does she need the money?"

Dad replied, "I can't answer that question because I do not know the answer. She has taught piano lessons since I was a child. Like you, I am not sure if she enjoys it. However, the students keep coming back, so I guess she is nice to the students and their parents."

"While we are on this subject, did she ever teach you to play piano?"

"No, she always said that it was not appropriate to teach your own children."

"I hope that she at least made cookies for you when you were a kid since she does not make cookies for me."

Dad did not reply, so I concluded that cookies were not available for him.

Mom said, "Grandpa Fritzie, her husband, was the real cook in Dad's family, so I bet he baked bread, cakes, and cookies. He died when you were 2 years old, so you don't remember him. He loved you so much and thought that you looked a lot like his daughter, Henrietta. She died at age 6, when Dad was 9."

By this time, we were almost home, so the conversation ended. The snow was starting to fall. I loved watching the snow fall in the streetlights. This ride ended the two-day celebration of Thanksgiving for another year.

Chapter 7

As December merged into the holiday season, the guest list for Christmas Eve dinner followed the same pattern as Thanksgiving. Dad and I would pick up Aunt Clara and Grandma Joanna while Mom finished preparing for dinner. I was always puzzled that they never brought Christmas gifts to exchange before dinner.

While in the car, I asked Dad, "Why don't Grandma and Aunt Clara ever bring gifts to the dinner?"

He replied, "During the Great Depression, I was a child. We lived in Denver. We had little money and food. My dad used to buy dented cans without labels for two cents. Once a week, my mom opened the dented can, and whatever was in the can was what we had for dessert. Often, the food was spoiled because the can was dented, so mom threw it away. Other times, it was green beans or some other vegetable. Rarely, it was canned fruit, like peaches or pears. That was always a wonderful and yummy surprise. For Christmas, my dad would save a little money to buy fresh oranges and apples. When my sister was alive, he would give us one peppermint candy stick and one piece of chocolate candy. When my sister passed away at age 6, I was nine years old. After she passed away, my parents never recovered, and we never celebrated Christmas again. I guess that is why Grandma never gives you a gift, and that is not fair to you. I can't change it. I hope you can understand."

"I understand, Dad, but I feel so sorry for you. It seems like you lost your little sister and Christmas in the same year. Your mom never recovered, and the death of her husband when I was a baby added to her life of grief. That is so sad."

"Yes, Kay, that is exactly what happened."

"How did you recover because you seem to really love Christmas?"

"Well, after the war, I met your mom. I learned a powerful lesson about life from her. During the war, her fiancée was killed, and within a few months, her younger brother died in a London air raid. Your mother taught me how to enjoy life in spite of tragedy and grief."

"I know her life story, but now I understand it by what you said."

By then, Dad was parking the car in front of Grandma Joanna's house. A repeat of the Thanksgiving pickup took place.

By the time we got home with Aunt Clara and Grandma Joanna, mom had the dining room table set with the special Swedish plates used only for Christmas Eve dinner. My parents inherited these unique dishes from Dad's father. There were no salad plates, because salad was never served at this meal. The dinner plates were white and covered with hand-painted beautiful roses, the color between red and magenta with the leaves being spring green. A white tablecloth was used with Christmas green tapered candles in clear glass holders. Since the meal was white and dark purple, the plate with food presented nicely. The plates were never used for any other meal because other "regular" meals have many colors that would distract from the rose pattern.

The Swedish Christmas Eve menu included boiled potatoes, lutfisk (a dish made from aged and salted whitefish, notorious for its gelatinous texture and pungent odor, although cherished by enthusiasts), pickled herring, and lingonberries.

Homemade baking powder biscuits rounded out the offerings. Lutfisk required extensive preparation, soaking in cold water for five or six days with daily water changes. Additionally, meticulous care was necessary during the cooking and serving of lutfisk, as any residue left on plates, cutlery, or frying pans had to be immediately removed, lest it become nearly impossible to clean. Interestingly, sterling silverware would corrode permanently if it came into contact with lutfisk, making stainless steel a requirement for this dish.

I dreaded this meal, but I was only required to eat potatoes, biscuits, and lingonberries. Mom made sure that I had a substantial late lunch on Christmas Eve. However, as I grew older, I gained respect for carrying on the family tradition brought to the U.S. from Sweden long ago.

At dinner, the conversation was pleasant and mostly focused on the weather since it was snowing outside. As usual Aunt Clara would talk about her world travel experiences when she was in her early 30s. This year, for some unknown reason, she chose to describe Diwali, the festival of lights, in India.

She said, "Diwali is a 5-day celebration of good over evil and light over darkness. The children that I cared for on the yacht were excited because we docked on the first day of Diwali at the port on the Arabian Sea near the city of Bombay. The children had been on the yacht for several days, so they were excited to get on land and celebrate any holiday. Diwali is especially fun for children because vendors give children sweets. The biggest celebration of fireworks happens on the third day of Diwali to signify the victory of light over darkness. The children had never seen such a big display of fireworks, but the crowds in the streets were frightening for the children who lived on a quiet yacht. Mostly the fireworks were on the street, like sparklers, rather than the fireworks in the sky, like what we know now.

 Their father, the captain of the yacht, had business in Bombay for a few days. It was my duty to keep track of the children while teaching them the history of India. Since it was my first visit to Bombay, I needed to learn fast so I could teach the children. All I remember was the most prominent building in Bombay was the Prince of Wales Museum of Western India. It was built around 1914 but was used as a military hospital at that time, so there were no museums to show the children. We mostly walked the streets and shopped in the street markets."

For dessert, we enjoyed sliced fruitcake accompanied by a small cup of hot Glogg, the traditional Swedish winter wine. A cup of hot coffee, sans sugar or cream, rounded out this delightful finale.

After dinner, the table was clear again. It was getting dark, and Grandma and Aunt Clara were getting anxious to go home. So, Dad retrieved their coats, scarves, and purses while Mom and I went to the bathroom and got our coats. I was always amazed that the ladies never used the bathroom. Dad grabbed his coat as we walked into the garage.

As before, I sat in the middle of the backseat with Aunt Clara on my left and Grandma Joanna on my right. It was snowing with big flakes, so I was glad that I had a great view through the front windshield. Dad took the long way to their houses so they could enjoy seeing the holiday lights on 16th Street, the Civic Center, the Capital Building, and a few of the surrounding neighborhoods. This view was always my favorite part of Christmas Eve, especially when it was snowing. Dad went to Aunt Clara's house first, and as usual he walked her up the front porch steps, down the long hallway, and into her dining room and then returned to the warm car.

The next stop was Grandma Joanna's house. She has no steps to her front porch, so she has easy access to her front door. Dad unlocked and opened the door. After she was settled with her coat off, he returned to the car.

As soon as he shut the car door, he looked at his watch and said, "If we can find a parking place, we will be on time for the 9:00 p.m. Christmas Eve Mass."

Fortunately, the church was close to Grandma's house, and Dad found a parking place in the lot across from the church. My parents never mentioned leaving the house and taking them home to get to Mass on time since that side of the family is Augustinian Lutheran, even though neither Aunt Clara nor Grandma Joanna ever attended any Lutheran services. Another example of what never made sense to me as a kid.

Back at home, the cozy ambiance of the Christmas Eve Mass lingered as Dad kindled a warm, crackling fire in the fireplace.

Eager to get into the holiday spirit, I hurriedly changed into my soft, comfortable pajamas. The familiar scent of freshly cut pine from our Christmas tree filled the air, mixing with the warmth from the fireplace. It was a feeling of pure comfort and contentment.

Meanwhile, Mom and Dad decided to indulge in their favorite winter drink, Old Fashion. They carefully prepared it, mixing bourbon, bitters, and water and garnishing it with an orange slice and a cocktail cherry. The clink of ice cubes in the glasses added a touch of sophistication to the evening. With their drinks in hand, they settled into their favorite armchairs.

As for me, exhaustion from the busy day began to catch up. In the spirit of the season, I took a moment to prepare a plate of cookies and a handful of carrots for Santa and his reindeer. Placing them by the twinkling lights of the Christmas tree, I felt a childlike excitement building within me.

With my preparations complete, I approached Dad and Mom, each with a drink in hand. I gave them both a warm, affectionate "good night" hug, feeling the love and warmth that this special evening brought to our family.

Tomorrow, we would be off to Grandpa and Grandma's house for an early dinner, continuing our cherished family traditions and celebrating the holiday season together.

Chapter 8

In 1971, the summer before I left for college, my parents visited Aunt Clara to help install a new toilet. Not doing anything exciting myself that Saturday afternoon, I agreed to come along, figuring it might be the last time I see Aunt Clara for a while.

Once we arrived, Mom and Dad began unloading the new toilet, pipes, and supplies from the truck onto the front porch while Aunt Clara and I watched and stayed out of the way. After they carried the toilet and supplies through the dining room and into the bathroom that was located to the left of the kitchen, Aunt Clara and I went into the house. Immediately, Dad and Mom got to work with the plumbing repair job, even with the window open, the house was hot with no breeze.

Inside, a small table fan was all but worthless and whirred on. Aunt Clara told me to sit in a specific chair at the dining table. I guess I had graduated from the trunk.

As usual, Aunt Clara sat at the head of the table, and, as usual, newspapers, sketch pads, and an old radio littered the space. I saw pencil drawings of famous baseball players on a few of the sketch pads. I remembered that she listened to baseball games on the radio when she was not listening to Oral Roberts' evangelical sermons.

Knowing it was going to be a long afternoon, I tried to start a conversation.

"Aunt Clara, what newspapers do you read daily?"

"Five newspapers: Denver Post, Rocky Mountain News, New York Times, Wall Street Journal, and the Washington Post," she said automatically. Then, remembering herself after a moment, she added, "Don't be so nosy."

But I was not about to sit in silence for several hours. I thought maybe a different approach might fare better.

"When I was younger, sometimes at Thanksgiving Dinner, you would tell stories about your world travels. Do you remember that? About the yacht and the captain and the seven children. Could you tell me more about those travels, please? I think I want to travel someday like you did. How did you get the opportunity to meet a yacht captain, anyway?"

"Oh, Kay, that was so many years ago." But her face lit up as she spoke, and I knew I'd hit one of the few sweet spots she had. Then she started to really talk.

"It was January 1918. I was teaching in an elementary school and had been teaching it for eight years by then. And I was getting tired of the day-to-day routine."

"My parents were always trying to get me married off around then. You see, they had moved to Denver around then, into this house that we are sitting in right now." She gestured vaguely to the space before us.

"They were always talking about how all my siblings were married and had children. And even though I told them I had no interest in marrying at the time, they kept trying to set me up with the sons of their wealthy socialite friend. Among the Denver rich, in those days, everyone assumed that an unmarried daughter over the age of 25 had to have something wrong with her. So much so that no man wanted to marry her."

"Anyway, I got home from teaching one day in January and my mother told me that I should go and attend a Denver Library celebration that evening with them. Of course, I didn't want to go, but I also did not want to argue with my mother about not being married for the hundredth time, either. So, I gave in and went upstairs and put on my favorite dress.

"Much to my surprise, I had a good time. After I got away from my parents, that is. And that's when I met Captain Greg Williams. We were both waiting in line for drinks."

She rightened herself in her seat as though to emphasize the importance of this next part.

"Kay, let me tell you that Greg was a handsome and well-dressed gentleman. He introduced himself very politely, and we decided to keep talking even after we had got our drinks. For most of the evening, we discussed his travel adventures. He had traveled extensively in Europe, Asia, and some of Africa. I was impressed when he told me that he spoke English, French, and Chinese fluently. He described his childhood as one long adventure. His parents owned a large import business in New York City, so they traveled six months every year. He attended a boarding school in Massachusetts. During the winter and summer break, he traveled with his parents. I remember that he got interested in sailing while attending Harvard. After his parents retired, he continued the family business."

"Was it love at first sight?"

"No, he seemed nice, and he was so handsome, but I was not sure about falling in love with a man after knowing him for a few hours."

"We exchanged addresses before I left. He lived in the Mile High District, too, a few blocks away from my parents' place."

"On the way home, I told my parents that I had met an interesting gentleman. Of course, my father knew it was Greg right away. They had various civic associations together, probably. My mother commented that they had noticed Greg and I having a long conversation but that they figured it was best to leave me be and see where it went. I didn't talk to men nearly as much as most other single women my age did, mind you."

I nodded understandingly.

"Over the following weeks, Greg and I got dinner together a few times. He told me about how his wife, Sarah, had recently passed away and how their seven children had since moved away to live with his parents in Los Angeles. He often talked about how he planned to take his children on a sailing trip across the Pacific on his yacht. I quickly shared my lifelong dream of traveling the world after I learned of the yacht, telling Greg about all the places I'd go if I had a yacht of my own."

"After a few more weeks, he invited me to the Brown Palace Hotel for a fancy dinner. God, I was so afraid that he was going propose to me that night, Kay. Of course, I liked him, but the thought of spending the rest of my life with him and his seven children was beyond my imagination."

Nevertheless, I used the invitation to go shopping for a beautiful new outfit. I got my mother to buy it for me, too, by telling her what the occasion was. They were all but sure that I was going to come home an engaged woman that night."

Thankfully, Greg did ask a question at dinner, but it was not "Will you marry me?" Instead, he asked me if I would like to homeschool his seven children on the yacht during their Pacific voyage. He assured me that I'd get a generous salary and a private suite of my own, among many other things. He had a full-time chef and housecleaner.

"I was so excited about the offer, and not because it had come in place of a marriage proposal, either. But I needed time to think about it, and I told Greg this before our dinner ended. Greg said they were departing in three months, in December, which meant I'd have ample time to resign from my teaching position if I decided to come."

"He mentioned that I wouldn't meet his children until they reached Los Angeles. Like I said before, they were living with his wife's parents at that point, going to some private school I'd never heard of. He explained to me how he didn't want to start sailing until the end of their school year. Greg assured me that I would love his children many times. He also explained that his yacht was dry-docked in Honolulu, so we would fly from Denver to Los Angeles to pick up the children and proceed to Hawaii.

I told my parents about Greg's offer when I got home, and they said it was a wonderful opportunity for me. I could see that they were disappointed that the night had not ended in a marriage proposal and a large diamond

Chapter 8

engagement ring, but the thought that I might still become Mrs. Greg Williams if I went on this trip seemed to cheer them up a little. Plus, they knew I had always wanted to travel the world. They probably thought that he'd get attached to me if we were stuck on his yacht together long enough.".

"I had less than one week to make the decision."

My parents came into the dining room just as Aunt Clara finished that sentence, covered in sweat and clearly exhausted.

"We were able to finish it all," my dad proudly announced. "And we put in some new plumbing pipes, too, on top of the new toilet."

We all sat around the table for a few minutes after that, awkwardly talking about nothing while my mom and dad took turns refilling their glasses of water. Finally, my dad said,

"Well, we probably should be getting home now."

He paused after this, giving Aunt Clara one final opportunity to say thank you for all their hard work.

"I'll use my neighbor's phone to call you when it breaks again."

My dad looked like he was going to say something for a moment, but whatever, it never came out.

"Come on, Kay, let's head out. It's too hot here for me. Bye, Clara!"

We headed out together. Aunt Clara watched me go but said nothing.

Chapter 9

Before returning to college, I decided to visit Aunt Clara. She was getting up in age, and I wasn't certain if this might be my last chance to see her. It was a warm and sunny afternoon in early September. The idea of visiting her on my own was intriguing.

As I drove without Dad providing directions, I pondered, "Will she recognize me? How would she react to me without my parents?"

The leaves were beginning to change into crimson and golden hues. In my mind, it was a perfect day. However, my thoughts vacillated between anxiety and optimism.

"As a child, I was fearful of Aunt Clara. Her house was creepy and the mere thought of visiting her caused me anxiety. I was older now and willing to take the risk of visiting. I wanted to learn for myself that she was really a kind, old woman, and my childhood memories were without merit."

I thought, "She might enjoy driving to a nearby coffee shop, sitting outside, and having a cup of tea together. However, I couldn't call ahead because she still didn't have a telephone, a relic of a bygone era."

I parked on Lincoln Street, not far from the front of her aging home. As I stepped out of my car, a wave of anxiety washed over me, a feeling eerily like the unease I experienced as a young child.

I scolded myself internally, thinking, "For God's sake, I'm 19 years old. Why am I so nervous about visiting this elderly woman who happens to be my great-aunt? Get over yourself."

Summoning my courage and determination, I climbed the creaking wooden stairs and pushed the button to ring Aunt Clara's doorbell, which sounded more like a buzzer. As I waited, my eyes drifted to two rusted mailboxes hanging in the same spot on the wide door frame. They had been there as far back as I could remember, and I wondered how long they'd been witnesses to the comings and goings of Aunt Clara's life.

After receiving no response, I rang the doorbell again. This time, I heard the familiar sound of Aunt Clara's footsteps echoing down the long hallway from her front door. A knot formed

Chapter 9

in my throat as the anticipation grew. The door opened a crack, and Aunt Clara peered out, trying to ascertain who could possibly be visiting her. She stared at me for several seconds before recognition finally crossed her face.

"What are you doing here?" she asked, her tone wary and a touch hostile.

"I was in the neighborhood and thought I'd stop by on this beautiful afternoon," I replied, attempting to sound casual.

"I walked to the grocery this morning, so I don't need to go outside this afternoon. What do you want? I hope you're not going to ask for money because I won't give you any money. Did your parents tell you to come visit me?" Aunt Clara's suspicion was palpable.

"Aunt Clara, I had an errand downtown, so I thought you might like to get out in this nice weather. It sounds like I interrupted you, so I'll leave now. I'm sorry that I disturbed your afternoon."

With that, Aunt Clara closed the door, and I heard her footsteps receding down the hall. As I walked back to my car, I couldn't shake the lingering feeling of tension from our encounter.

Throughout the day, I couldn't stop thinking about Aunt Clara and that brief conversation. One question haunted me: What had happened in her life to make her so bitter and angry? As a child, I had always found her intimidating, but now I couldn't help but see her as a damaged and broken elderly woman. But the mystery remained: why? This encounter left a lasting impression on me, sparking a curiosity that I couldn't easily put to rest.

Chapter 10

The kitchen phone rang.

Mom was calling from Texas and reported, "Kay, Aunt Clara was admitted to the Denver General Hospital yesterday. Her neighbor noticed several newspapers were piled on her front porch. Mrs. Beatty knocked on the door, but there was no answer. She ran back home to get Clara's house key. She unlocked the door and found her on the kitchen floor. It had been two days."

"Yikes, Mom. What was her condition when she found her?"

"Mrs. Beatty said that she was weak but conscious. Of course, she called an ambulance. Clara asked her, 'What took you so long? I guess that I slipped and fell. I am thirsty, and I soiled myself.'"

"That's Clara," I thought to myself.

"I think; the surgery was yesterday." Mom continued, "Would you please go to the hospital and check on her?"

I said, "Yes, sure. I will ask Linda if she can babysit Scott for a few hours."

I located Aunt Clara's room after a quick stop with the front desk receptionist. I took a deep breath as I entered Aunt Clara's room. I had no idea what to expect.

She was awake, looking out the window.

"Aunt Clara, it's me, Kay. I came to visit you. How are you feeling?"

"Thanks for coming," she said in a tone of voice that was about as close to thankful as I had ever heard from her or a voice that sounded more bored/annoyed/absent-minded than thankful.

"I'm glad that my neighbor, Mrs. Beatty, found me on the floor of my kitchen. Did they tell you that an ambulance brought me here?"

I nodded silently.

The doctors told me I have a minor hip fracture. They could not do surgery because of my age, so it is wrapped. I have to move around a lot because they say I'll get pneumonia if I don't move. It hurts, and the exercise makes the pain worse." She grimaced a little then as though the thought of exercising brought her pain.

Chapter 10

"Are you getting enough pain medication?"

"No, but there's no point in asking. They've ignored me ever since I got here."

As we were talking, a woman entered her room.

"Hello, Miss Schattinger. My name is Jannette Coleman, and I've been assigned to be your case manager. Your doctor wrote your discharge order for you to be transported to a rehabilitation nursing facility in a few days. You will stay there for physical therapy to gain strength before returning home."

"Where are you putting me? May I refuse to go to such a place?"

The lady gave Aunt Clara a placating smile, one I could tell she'd spent years perfecting.

"Your doctor thinks you would be safer at home following a few weeks in of physical therapy in a rehabilitation facility."

"Hogwash. I fell in the kitchen and lived for two days on the cold floor. Just because I am old, I can care for myself at home. I am tough and sturdy. Tell that doctor to write the order so I can go home. And you get out of my room."

The case manager left.

"Is there anything that you want me to do before I leave?" I asked Aunt Clara.

"I thought that you were a nurse. Are you going to help me? Do you understand that I want to go home and not be transported to a nursing home against my wishes? Please help me."

"Let's see how you progress over the next few days. Before I leave, would you like for me to get you anything?"

"Do you think that you could bring a sandwich with some real meat? It's not that processed stuff they have here. I want lettuce and tomato, too. Tell them I want toasted pumpernickel bread. No mayonnaise or mustard. And a good cup of black coffee. No, make it two cups of coffee. No cream and sugar. That stuff is poison and will kill you. I know that I have told you that information before."

I took her request as a positive sign. At least she realized that I was willing to get her a sandwich. She seemed in her element by giving me orders like that.

About 20 minutes later, I returned to her room with her sandwich and two cups of coffee from the hospital cafe.

Chapter 10

"I have your sandwich and coffee. Do you want it now?"

"Yes, of course, I want it now. Why else would I have sent you?" She nabbed the food out of my hand savagely. "All they have here is their canned and processed food, and I know I've told you many, many times that I walk to the grocery every day to get fresh food. I'd rather starve than eat what they try to give me here. And now I am stuck here," she finished with a pout.

"Here, I can help you. Let's start with the coffee, then I'll unwrap your sandwich for you."

She waved away my outstretched helping hand like a pesky summer mosquito.

"My hip is broken, not my arms. I can unwrap my sandwich and drink my coffee without you making it any harder for me."

I sat silently in the chair near her bed, trying not to disturb her as she ate.

"I'm finished. Take this trash out for me."

She paused for a moment, then added, "Thank you for bringing me some semi-real food. It wasn't terrible."

"Do you need anything else before I go?"

"No," she said curtly. She followed this with a face that indicated a simple 'no' wasn't the only thing she wanted to say. "You should stay here, though. I want to talk to you about something."

Then she started to drift off into her memories. She was no longer talking to me but rather reminiscing by talking to herself.

"Did I ever tell you about how my mother broke her hip? She slipped on the kitchen floor, the same kitchen floor where I fell. Do you know that I live in the same house my parents lived in when they moved to Denver? My father tried to take care of her after the fall, but he couldn't do it. That's when I got a telegram telling me to come home immediately. I was in Paris when I got it. I was devastated by the telegram, but I had no choice. I was the only one of my siblings who didn't have a family or a spouse. I was the traveling spinster. But family takes care of family, so I resigned from the position where I took care of seven children."

Her tone started to get more and more nostalgic.

"I was a homeschool teacher on a yacht, and the captain purchased my tickets to get home.

Chapter 10

First, I went by train from Paris to the port city of LaHavre, France

. Then, I boarded a ferry to Southampton in England. I took the RMS Olympic transatlantic ship to New York City. Oh, that trip made many memories."

"The yacht captain had bought me a first-class ticket on that luxury ship. Nothing I could have ever afforded. I had a fabulous cabin and a private bathroom. It took about seven days to cross the Atlantic Ocean. I never wanted that trip to end. I remember the lavish Grand Staircase the ship had; it was three decks high. And food was as elegant as the fine porcelain dishes."

"What about your mom?" I interrupted.

"I'm getting there," she snapped back. "When I reached New York City, I took a train to Denver, Colorado. I think it took over a week to get home since there were so many stops along the way. The yacht captain could not purchase the train ticket for the U.S. trip, so my father wired money for the train ticket while I was stuck in New York City. I didn't want to go home by then. Home, taking care of my parents, was about the last place in the world I wanted to be."

I listened in silence. Clara had stopped talking and looked out the window. She looked tired, and I thought she might give up on her story and send me back home. But then she said,

"Back in those days, if you broke a hip, you had to stay in bed for months while it healed. My mother's hip never healed right, so she spent most of the rest of her life in bed. She occupied her time by sewing handmade quilts out of scraps of old silk dresses she'd never wear again. I took care of my bedridden mother at first, but then, the following year, my father was diagnosed with cancer. So, I never returned to Paris. I have never left Denver since the day I got off the train all those years ago."

Again, she looked out the hospital window. For the first time in my life, I saw her face relaxed. She looked back at me with an ever-so-small smile and said, "Do you think I need to go to that rehab place? Personally, I think that I can take care of myself."

"You'll probably need at least a few days of rehabilitation. You need to get your sense of balance back to prevent another fall."

Chapter 10

Later that afternoon, the hospital case manager arranged for her to be transported to a nearby rehabilitation nursing home in two days.

When I got back home, I called my parents to provide an update on her condition. They decided I had the situation under control and that there was no need for them to make the trip to Denver.

I waited a few days as she adjusted to the rehabilitation facility before visiting her. This time, I brought Scott with me. I thought Clara might enjoy meeting him.

After arriving, I was directed to Clara's private room. Several nurses smiled and asked to peek at the baby as we walked down the corridor to her room.

"Hi, Aunt Clara, I came to visit you. I brought Scott, your great, great nephew, so you can meet him."

Her face lit up. "May I hold him?"

"Of course."

"I have never held such a tiny baby," she said as I carefully handed over Scott. "Thanks for letting me meet him."

"How are you feeling?"

"I'm ready to get discharged if that's what you're asking. I went to a Bible Study session, but I had to teach for most of it since I was much more familiar with the chosen passages than the others. The kitchen fails to serve fresh fruit and vegetables. I'll die if I stay here another week."

"What did the doctor say?"

"He said that I need to stay another week." She shooed away this idea. "I'm planning to call a taxi tomorrow," she continued, "I'm sure I can finish recovering at home."

"Who will take care of you?"

"My neighbor will bring me food."

"You've called her since being here?"

She shook her head.

"Mrs. Beatty will help me if I ask for help. I know she will. Besides, I'll be motivated to get well, so I never have to come back here."

"I suppose that you know what's best for you."

"Yes, thanks for your vote of confidence." She yawned. "I'm starting to get tired, so you should probably leave. I appreciate your visit. I hope you and the baby will visit me when I'm back home."

Being a woman of strong will, Aunt Clara stuck to her plans. After getting dressed the next morning, she called a taxi and left, despite the doctor's strongly urging against it.

I visited her several times after that, always bringing Scott with me as well.

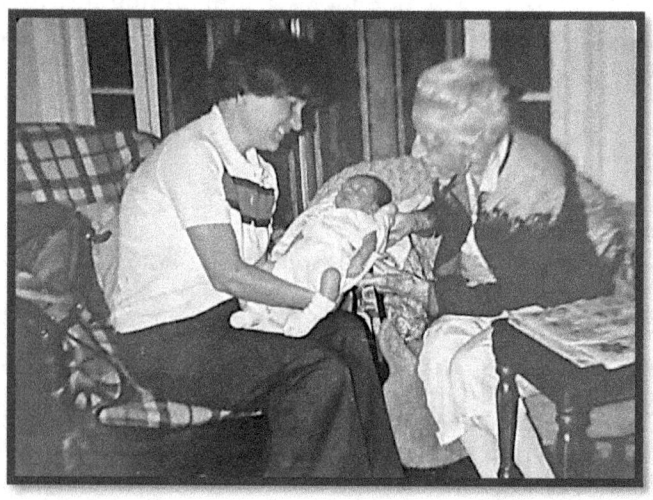

She did recover at home by using her self-designed therapy. She lived another three years.

The Spinster I Once Knew

Chapter 11

After living in Texas for several years, Mom and Dad retired to Denver to be closer to family and friends. One snowy morning after breakfast, Dad suggested to Mom that they check on Aunt Clara's furnace and plumbing since the weather had been extremely cold. Clara's old house often worried them due to her refusal to make repairs. Mom agreed, and washed the dishes while Dad prepared his toolbox. They drove to Clara's house quickly as the roads were plowed and traffic was light. On arrival, they noticed Clara's neighbor had shoveled the snow, making it easier to reach the house.

Dad knocked on the door but got no response, so they decided to check the back door. Seeing the kitchen light on, which Clara never left on when leaving the house, they grew concerned. Dad used his spare key to unlock the door, and they entered the freezing kitchen. The faint smell of something burnt lingered. They moved into the dim living room, where the cold air was visible with their breath, amplifying their worry about Clara's well-being.

Dad and Mom found Aunt Clara sleeping in the corner of her sparsely furnished living room, covered with thin blankets. When Dad tried to wake her, he realized she had died. He instructed Mom not to touch anything and to call the police. They went to Mrs. Beatty's house next door, but she wasn't home, so they used an old phone booth at the end of the street. Dad called the emergency number and reported Clara's death, providing her address and describing their green Ford pickup parked in front.

Within ten minutes, two police officers arrived. Dad unlocked the front door and explained how they had entered through the back. The officers confirmed Clara's death, suspecting she had passed away due to hypothermia. They collected contact information from Dad and Mom before allowing them to leave.

As Dad and Mom drove home, they reminisced about Aunt Clara's world travels. Clara's sister Joanna, Dad's mother, had died a few years ago, so there was no longer a need to check on both sisters. They agreed that Clara had lived a long, peaceful life. At home, they called two people. Dad called me, and Mom called Clara's neighbor, Mrs. Beatty, as there were no other relatives or friends to inform.

On Monday, the Medical Examiner confirmed Clara had frozen to death in her home, a common occurrence among the elderly during prolonged subzero temperatures. He explained that the elderly often turns off their furnaces to save money, but the cold overwhelms them in their sleep. Mom provided cemetery documents and later identified Clara's body, choosing Crown Hill Cemetery for her burial.

Mom then contacted Clara's estate attorney, Phil Bingham, to report Clara's death and set up an appointment to manage the estate. Mr. Bingham remembered them and acknowledged Fred Gustafson as the executor of Clara's estate.

Mom also inquired about cleaning Clara's house. Mr. Bingham advised against entering the house until they reviewed Clara's will, as it was still considered a crime scene. They scheduled a meeting for the following Thursday at 3:00 p.m.

Mom then called me to share the news. While I offered to help with the house cleaning, she assured me it wasn't necessary. Shortly after, the

Medical Examiner called to confirm that Clara had died of hypothermia and instructed them to wait for Clara's will before entering the house. Clara's body had been taken to Crown Hill Mortuary.

When Dad arrived home, they each had a Manhattan drink and discussed the next steps by the warmth of a fire.

The following week, they went to Phil Bingham's office. They were warmly greeted by the receptionist and waited in a conference room. Phil Bingham expressed his condolences and began reading Clara's last will and testament, ready to answer their questions afterward.

Phil Bingham read Clara Schattinger's will, revealing that her entire estate was bequeathed to Oral Roberts University, with permission for Dad and Mom to keep the contents of her house. This unexpected bequest reminded them of Clara's devotion to Oral Roberts, a charismatic televangelist that she listened to every day on the radio.

Dad asked about Clara's trustee banker, who was already finalizing her estate. Phil mentioned that Clara's estate was valued at over six million

Chapter 11

dollars. Shocked by the estate's value, Dad and Mom thanked Phil and left.

They went to the Medical Examiner's office, who confirmed they could enter Clara's house the next morning since there was no evidence of foul play. The police would remove the crime scene tape that afternoon.

The next morning, Dad and Mom prepared for a long day of sorting through Clara's household goods. After a hearty breakfast, they loaded their truck with moving boxes, tape, gloves, a toolbox, lunch, hot coffee, trash bags, and Dad's 35mm Kodak slide camera. Upon arriving at Clara's house, they donned gloves and entered the cold, dusty home. Dad briefly turned on the heat but quickly turned it off due to the dust.

Dad took photographs of each room before they began cleaning. They started with the kitchen and bathroom. Mom filled trash bags with spoiled food and dead plants while Dad gathered clean and filthy towels used soap bars, a comb, a brush, and a hand mirror from the bathroom. They packed silverware, utensils, dishes, and cookware into moving boxes for donation. They discovered most kitchen cupboards were empty except for a dead mouse in one drawer. These two rooms were cleared faster than anticipated.

Next, they moved to the living room/bedroom. Mom stripped the bed and threw all the linens into a trash bag. Dad removed the thin mattress, and they carried it out the back door, throwing it in the dumpster in the alley.

Back inside, they boxed all the dusty books and piles of paper on the bookshelves and the dining room table. They didn't try to sort anything; that would be done at home in the basement. Dad loaded a few table lamps and end tables into the truck bed from the sitting room at the front of the house.

While Dad loaded the truck, Mom managed to move the heavy trunk away from the wall. It had been covered with several wool blankets for probably fifty years. Mom remembered that Clara always had me sit on that trunk every time my parents visited.

Dad walked in and looked at the trunk without the blankets. It was in perfect condition.

Mom said, "I bet this trunk has been here in this same location since she arrived home after her world travels. Look, there are even some travel stickers on this end. I have always wondered what was in this trunk. Too bad that Kay is not with us today. She would love to witness the unveiling of the contents of the mystery trunk. I will call her tonight and reveal the secrets."

Dad started to fiddle with the lock when Mom found the key on the opposite end, hooked to the leather moving strap.

"Bingo, here is the key," proclaimed Mom.

Dad unlocked the trunk, and they both stared down as he lifted the creaky lid. It was filled with a wide assortment of boxes, books, files of papers, a carved wooden jewelry box, some silk dresses, coats, blankets, and shoes. They couldn't take the time now to open and sort the contents, so they closed the lid and decided to come back later to transport the travel trunk to their house. The truck bed was almost as full as it was.

Mom emptied the two unbroken drawers on the nightstand next to the bed. The items included a few handkerchiefs, a used jar of Vicks Vapor Rub, and a small bottle of lotion. The other drawer had an assortment of unmatched socks with holes in each heel or toe. Those items filled a portion of another plastic lawn trash bag. Mom found other items stashed behind the shoe rack and head of the bed that filled the remainder of the trash bag.

At this point, they stopped for lunch. They removed their gloves, washed their hands in the kitchen sink, and then went outside to sit in the cab of the truck to eat.

Mom said, "I don't know about you, but I worked up an appetite. We have more work ahead of us."

Dad agreed, "We won't finish today, but we have enough boxes in the truck to sort over the next few months."

Mom replied, "I want to get as much done today as possible. It needs so much repair. I am glad that we are not responsible for the repairs or the sale of the house. I am surprised that we got the contents of the house. It will be interesting to sort through her belongings."

Dad agreed, "I agree. She has used us as her servants for years without ever receiving even a thank you or payment for the supplies."

Mom said, "I agree. It is a relief that we no longer feel obligated to check on her and listen to her complaints. I am through with the whole situation. Do you want any more coffee before we go back to work?"

"Sure. You know that I never pass on a good cup of coffee."

Mom cleaned up the waxed paper from their sandwiches and cookies as Dad drank the last of the thermos coffee.

They went back into Clara's house. As they walked through the front door, Mom suggested that they go upstairs. Mom had never been allowed to scale the steps, and Dad's last memory of going upstairs was when he was an adolescent.

Dad nodded and said, "No one is here to stop us."

They reached the top of the stairs. There were four closed doors.

Dad said, "You choose. I can't remember anything."

Mom chose the first door on her right. She tried the door, but it was locked. Dad tried the other three doors. All the doors were locked.

Dad examined the doors and said, "All we need is an old-fashioned passkey. I might have one at home. Let's go downstairs and look in the drawers on Clara's desk. She might have kept the key there. It is worth a try."

They went downstairs, and Dad began his search for a passkey to open the upstairs doors. As luck would have it, he found such a key in the first drawer he looked in.

Dad held up the key and said, "Let's try this key upstairs. It might work."

They walked upstairs. Dad was correct. The passkey worked on the first door he tried. He held the door open to let Mom enter first.

She stopped and said, "You won't believe this. It is completely empty except for fifty years of dust."

Dad walked in and had the same reaction.

He asked, "Do you suppose she lied about having those male boarders? This explains why she never let anyone come upstairs; no one ever saw the borders, and this could be the reason why the mailbox is rusty. It was never used."

Mom and Dad went from room to room upstairs. Each room was empty, with not a single piece of furniture.

Chapter 11

Their last stop was the bathroom. It was the same as the other rooms. The toilet, sink, and shower were layered in dust. The faucet was rusted to the point of breaking off, and the toilet water had evaporated from the bowl and the tank.

Mom said, "Well, the upstairs certainly saved us hours of work hauling furniture and belongings down those steep stairs."

Dad replied, "It seems like the more we discover, the more questions remain unanswered."

"I agree. Let's get home and unload the boxes in the back of the truck before it gets any later."

"Good idea."

Relieved that there was no furniture to haul downstairs, they decided to head home and unload the truck. Exhausted, they carried the boxes into their basement and then relaxed with martinis after grilling hamburgers for dinner. They reflected on the many unanswered questions about Clara's life.

A few days later, they returned to Clara's house to collect the last items: a few lamps and the trunk. They carefully loaded the trunk into Dad's truck, protected it with a padded tarp, and dropped off the lamps at Goodwill. Despite the rain starting to sprinkle, they managed to unload the trunk at home and placed it in the basement bedroom that stored many historical documents in numerous large plastic containers from both sides of the family. The padded tarp was never removed, and the trunk remained unopened until after the death of my parents.

About fifteen years later, it was my turn to clean out my parents' house, including the garage, tool shed, attic, and basement. After Dad passed away, Mom and I sold his tools and most of the furniture. As Mom aged, she agreed to move into a retirement community. She had several large plastic bins filled with 3-ring binders of family history, photo albums, manila files of documents, and Aunt Clara's trunk encased in a padded tarp. Although Mom always intended to go through the bins, she never did before moving. I inherited the responsibility of moving the family history to my house, with the promise to sort through it and donate any valuable items to the Colorado Historical Society. Mom also asked that I examine the contents of Aunt Clara's trunk.

Soon after inheriting the bins and trunk, I started with the trunk, eager to solve a long-standing mystery. As a child, Aunt Clara always told me to sit on that trunk during visits, sparking my curiosity about its contents. Now, after waiting over 60 years later, I was finally going to uncover the mystery.

Carefully, I opened the heavy lid. The first few layers were blankets and two winter coats. Each item was neatly folded. Then, I removed several cardboard shoeboxes filled with trinkets, jewelry, lace handkerchiefs, silk scarves, and a few postcards. I removed two beautiful evening dresses, several pairs of dancing shoes, and a dainty sequined purse. As I was nearing the bottom, there were four books and two envelopes. I used scissors to cautiously open both envelopes. One had several photographs of what I assumed to be family and friends. A small, tattered, faded red book slithered out of the second envelope and the last item in the trunk. It read: *My Diary*.

PART THREE

"CLARA'S JOURNEY"

1. Denver, Colorado
2. Los Angeles
3. Honolulu, Hawaii
4. Tokyo, Japan
5. Yokohama Port, Japan
6. Seoul, Korea
7. Peking, China
8. Shanghai, China
9. Hong Kong, China
10. Manila, Philippines
11. Singapore
12. Port of Medan, Indonesia
13. Colombo, Sri Lanka
14. Calcutta, India
15. Delhi, India
16. Agra, India
17. Bombay, India
18. Cairo, Egypt

19. Bethlehem, Jerusalem
20. Haifa, Israel
21. Beirut, Lebanon
22. Athens, Port Piraeus, Greece
23. Constantinople, Turkey
24. Brindisi, Adriatic Sea, Italy
25. Naples, Italy
26. Pompeii, Italy
27. Rome, Italy
28. Florence, Italy
29. Venice, Italy
30. Milan, Italy
31. Alsace – Lorraine (border between France and Germany)
32. Paris, France
33. Le Havre, France
34. New York City, New York
35. Denver, Colorado

Chapter 12

Every Saturday morning, Clara had a ritual of taking the morning newspaper and walking to her favorite café. She always ordered coffee and a croissant while sitting outside if the weather was nice. On this Saturday, a young woman asked if she could join Clara, since there were no empty tables outside.

Clara glanced up and said, "Sure."

"Let me introduce myself. My name is Hazel Oldt."

"My name is Clara."

"I see that you are browsing the classified job ads. What kind of a job are you looking for?"

"Currently, I'm teaching at the Opportunity School, which focuses on the Montessori teaching methods. I have been there for a few years. I moved from Fairplay to Denver," Clara told her new companion. "My teaching position came with a good salary, and I love living in Denver. I lived in a boardinghouse for a while, but then my parents retired and bought a house close to here. I'm tired of living with my parents, and I am sick of teaching altogether. What I really want to do is travel the world." She was willing to share her dreams with about anyone willing to listen to her.

"Well, if you want to travel, and I want to travel, then let's go travel!"

Clara was taken aback by Hazel's straightforwardness, and understandably so. Clara had moved back in with her parents after living in the boarding house while teaching for a few years. Additionally, she had spent the last few weeks scouting out apartments. Now, right before she was not only someone encouraging me to abandon all these ideas but declaring she'd come with Clara to wherever she wished to go.

"Is it really that easy?" she asked skeptically.

"Yes," Hazel replied with a confident smile. "As long as you have money, the world is yours."

Curious to know more about her new friend and possibly future travel companion, Clara said, "You said your name is Hazel, right? Could you tell me a little more about yourself?"

"OK," Hazel began, sitting up in her chair. "I'm 29. I was born in 1892 in River Rouge, Michigan, in a family of nine siblings. I grew up in

Chapter 12

I was the second child, but my older sister died at age two. Another child, Paul, died before he turned one. Dorothy and Mildred were twins, but they died soon after birth. My parents are James and Nora Oldt. My mother spent most of her married life either pregnant or grieving. My dad worked in a factory and was mostly depressed."

"Hold on, hold on," Clara interrupted. "I asked you to tell me about yourself, not your whole family tree. I'm not planning on traveling the world with your depressed dad."

Hazel smiled at this comment, though Clara had meant what she said in no joking sense.

"Alright. Well, what else is there? After I graduated from high school, I knew I wanted to get out of Michigan. I didn't want the life my parents had, so I moved to Chicago to experience the big city life, kind of like you said you want to do. In Chicago, I landed a job with a secretarial typing pool. I had to lie about my age to get the job, but I typed fast enough to keep them from asking questions like that. I shared a room in a boardinghouse with a bunch of other young, single women. The landlady was a good cook, so dinner was worth putting up with the lousy roommate."

"I saved up some money once I finally settled down in the city, even though I went to the local bars almost every night. Hmmm, what else? Oh, I got involved with a wealthy married businessman. I met him in a bar. He took me back to his hotel that night after claiming he was on a business trip. The truth was he always had that hotel room in case he got lucky at some bar. I guess that I was his trophy for that night. However, we met at the bar for several nights; then, he insisted that we skip the bar and meet at the hotel every night. He was old but nice, and I guess you could say I became his mistress for a while, which was... interesting. He was terrible in bed, but he paid me well, so I never said anything about it. He gave me more money per night than I earned in a week at work, and I put those earnings in the bank, too."

Hazel winked at Clara, who said nothing and gave her only the most stoic of looks. But Hazel kept on, undeterred.

"After he disappeared for a few weeks, I saw in the newspaper that he had died suddenly. There was a big article about him right on the front page. Maybe you've heard of him. Henry Whittinger, the Chicago railroad tycoon. I was glad that he did not die when he was having sex with me. That would have been strange. I can't imagine explaining that to the police."

Clara shook her head.

"I guess that makes sense. Hell, I didn't know who he was until he died, and I was sleeping with him!" Hazel laughed. "Oh well. Life goes on. After that, I left Chicago, and spent some time in Omaha, Kansas City, Oklahoma City, all over the place really. Then I moved to Denver, and now here I am, meeting you."

Despite brief responses and a continually aloof look on her face, Clara couldn't help but be fascinated by Hazel's story. Here was someone who had done everything Clara had only dreamt of doing. "Do you have a job in Denver?" she asked, trying to flatten her tone to conceal her budding excitement.

"No," Hazel admitted. "I've only been here a week. I have found a boardinghouse, though, so I do have housing and one meal a day."

"Aren't you worried about using up all your savings? I mean, you are looking for a job, aren't you?"

"No, I'm not worried about any of that. I'm sure something will come up. In fact, I'd say something *has* come up now." Hazel gave Clara a knowing grin, and it took a moment for Clara to realize she was referencing their own conversation. Clara couldn't help but smile at herself, if only for a moment.

"Maybe we can figure this out together," Clara said. Hazel's stories had sparked in Clara a growing sense of excitement about the future and the possibilities it held.

"We both want to travel, and we're both in a new place. Why not make the most of it?"

Hazel smiled warmly.

Clara returned her smile with the same warmth and eagerness, and so, their journey began then and there, with nothing more than the implicit agreement that they would unite in the pursuit of their shared dream and with the determination to see it through.

With a newfound optimism, Hazel reached into her bag and pulled out the newspaper.

"I was actually looking at the classified ads in today's paper when I noticed you. Would you mind looking at the ads with me and trying to help me see where I can get a job?"

Chapter 12

"A job?" Clara asked in astonishment. "I thought we were going to travel the world together. Why do you need a job in Denver to do that?"

"Do you remember what I said earlier? 'As long as you have money, the world is yours,'? Well, if we want to travel, we're going to need some money to do so, and my Chicago funds have about run out, to tell the truth. Besides, you have a good teaching job for now."

Seeing the disappointment in Clara's eyes, Hazel added, "It will only be temporary. Until we get enough money saved up or something else comes up. We'll be out of here in no time."

"Alright," said Clara, not even attempting to conceal the gloom that had come over her following the delay of her dream. "Let me see that."

Hazel handed her the newspaper, then asked a nearby waiter for two more coffees while Clara scoured the classified section she had now spread across the table.

"All these jobs are boring and have low pay," she said with a frown. "Do you have any skills besides your typing experience?"

"Oh please," Hazel said, "I've never been to a city that didn't need a good typist somewhere. You must not be looking at it right. Here, gimme."

"Hold on a second," Clara said.

"C'mon, give it back. I've looked through a hundred classifieds before, Clara. I know what to do. Gimme."

So, with an exasperated sigh, Clara handed over the newspaper. Then she waited five, ten, fifteen minutes, polishing off her coffee before speaking again.

"Nothing?"

"Nothing," Hazel repeated, frustrated. "This is ridiculous. I've never seen a classified without any typing jobs, and in a city this big, too! And I need to find something this week – I don't want to dip into what little there is of my travel savings if I can help it."

The two continued their search for another twenty minutes, handing the classified back and forth while trying to figure out how much they could stretch out Hazel's résumé if that's what it came down to. In the end, they decided to call it a day without picking out a single job opening for Hazel to apply to.

Chapter 12

"How about we meet up here again on Saturday?" Hazel said eventually. "I'll bring the new classified then, and I'm sure there will be some sort of typist opening in it."

And so, they agreed to come back Saturday morning to continue their search. Clara reached out her hand to say goodbye to Hazel.

"I'm glad we met," she said. Hand extended.

Hazel brushed the hand aside, squeezing Clara in a bear hug instead.

"I'm glad we met, too," Hazel said as she squeezed her tighter. "And don't you worry about a thing, Clara? We'll be on our way out of here before you know it!"

Hazel let go of Clara, scooped up her purse, and headed off.

"And remember, meet here Saturday at 10:30! Don't you forget!"

Clara waved goodbye, unable to say much of anything before Hazel turned behind a building and was gone from sight, slipping out of her world as quickly as she had slipped into it.

Saturday arrived. Clara had got to the café around 9:30 to browse the classified ads in the early morning paper. Though she didn't want to admit it, she was a bit nervous Hazel wouldn't show up. After all, I wasn't meeting someone like her, who promised to help whisk you away after a day together, almost too good to be true? So, when she finally looked up and saw Hazel running towards her, waving a newspaper excitedly, she smiled more in relief than in excitement.

"Clara, I found it!" Hazel shouted.

She pulled out a chair from the table Clara sat at and said, through intermittent heavy breathing, "Wait until you see what I found. You're going to be so happy. Look at this ad. Can you believe it? Can you?"

Clara read the ad. Then she read it again and then a third time.

"This is too good to be true," she said.

"Of course, it's true. Why would they pay for a false ad?"

"Let me read it again. 'Looking for single women over the age of 25 to work on cruise ships. Multiple positions available.'"

"It's like the universe brought us together to do this," Hazel interrupted. "I mean, what are the odds?"

But Clara only kept on reading the advertisement.

"'Write a letter describing your work experience and availability to travel for six months. Travel costs to and from Hawaii are not included in the employment. Mail to: Pacific Cruise Corporation, General Post Office, Box 1247, Los Angeles, California.'"

She put the newspaper down and stared at it for a moment in a sort of stupor. Then she looked up at Hazel.

"OK, let's think about this for a minute. There's got to be a catch, right?"

Hazel shook her head.

"That's what I thought too. But I've read it repeatedly, and I can't find one. I mean, the only thing that doesn't make sense to me is the California address if we're going to be working in Hawaii."

"They probably use the California address because it would take months to get a letter to Hawaii."

"Yes, that's got to be it!" cried Hazel. "I knew there was something about you, Clara. I don't talk about traveling with just anyone, but I knew from the moment we first started talking there was something special about you. You're smart, aren't you?"

"Only the smartest in my family," said Clara with a haughty smirk.

"So, you're in? Going to a big city and traveling across most of the Pacific Ocean are two different levels of travel, you know. You don't feel like I'm forcing you to do this, do you?"

"You'd have to force me not to pass up an offer like this," Clara affirmed her friend.

"Well then, to Hawaii, we must go!" Hazel declared. "If you get hired, could you afford travel expenses? And do you have any idea how much it would cost to get there?"

"Let's say we took a train from Denver to Los Angeles, then a ship from Los Angeles to Honolulu. We need to go to the Union Station and

Chapter 12

ask the agent. They ought to know how to get people to different places."

"First, we should write our letters," said Clara. She was beginning to see she would need to be the level-headed one of the pair, considering what she'd seen of Hazel's inclination to rush headfirst into about anything so far.

"I have a typewriter back in my boarding room," said Hazel.

"Let's handwrite our letters first and then type and mail them after."

"Clara, are you as excited as I am? Think of it. Hawaii!"

Clara grinned and nodded, then pulled out a tablet of paper from her purse. "I have a pad of paper and two pencils on me, funny enough. If you want, we could write the letters now, or we could wait until –"

Hazel snatched several pieces of paper out of Clara's hand before she could even finish the sentence.

And with that, they began writing and rewriting their letters over the next few days, comparing each other's letters over a morning coffee and editing them once more later that night. They then went to the boarding house to type out the letters. Even with Hazel's expertise, it took several attempts to type error-free letters and envelopes on high-quality stationery. Still, neither of them complained when the other pointed out a mistake and said they'd have to try again, no matter how small and frivolous it was. They wanted the cruise line employer to believe that they were excellent candidates for this opportunity.

They continued to meet at the café after finally mailing the finished letters, chatting excitedly about their soon-to-be upcoming adventure. Caught up in each other's excitement over the fantasies of open seas and tropical islands, neither of them doubted for a moment whether they'd get the jobs or not. Each afternoon, they checked and double-checked their mailboxes, thinking about the endless possibilities throughout the night.

"We need to figure out what we're going to pack in our trunks," said Hazel one day over coffee.

"We haven't even gotten the jobs yet, Hazel, and besides, I have lesson plans to prepare and papers to grade for my students. Don't you think

Chapter 12

that would be getting a bit ahead of ourselves?" Clara said. It had been two weeks since they mailed their letters, and, unlike her friend, Clara's excitement had begun to dwindle a bit. It had been fun to mail the letters and fantasize about Hawaii every day over coffee, but there was a very real chance they could never even hear back from the company. Then what would they do?

"We need to plan, so when the letters arrive, we're ready," said Hazel. "Oh, and have you told your parents yet? My parents don't know that I'm in Denver, so sending them a postcard from Hawaii wouldn't be too big of a surprise, I don't think."

"No, I'm not going to tell them. I plan to tell them that I am going to Hawaii. They don't need to know the details; besides, they ask too many questions."

"All I've done this week is think about packing," said Hazel, eager to steer the conversation back toward her chosen topic. "I'm thinking I'll need a sewing kit so that I can make dresses for fancy events, shoes for work, walking, and dancing. Oh, and sexy lingerie, too, in case there are any cute co-workers, and sweaters and coats. I started making a list."

"Really, the first thing on your list is a sewing kit?"

"Well then, tell me what it is *you* are planning on bringing?"

Clara sighed.

"I haven't thought about taking anything yet. I was planning on crossing that bridge when we got there. But if I had to guess off the top of my head, I'd probably pack a stack of books, plenty of paper, envelopes, and a diary, plus year-round clothing and herbal medicine. Keep in mind that the pandemic is still lingering around the world."

"Clara, you are so practical. Is that why you rarely smile? Take some fun items."

This conversation became a daily event after Clara finished teaching for the next several weeks. Hazel liked to talk about it because she kept discovering new items she'd need to pack for when the letter came, and Clara liked to talk about it because it kept her mind distracted from the ever-growing possibility they wouldn't need to pack anything at all. After a while, even Hazel's enthusiasm died down a little bit, and soon they started agreeing to come to coffee every day when

Chapter 12

Clara finished teaching and Saturdays as they had done the second time they met.

They had promised shortly after mailing their letters out that they would bring the responses they got to the cafe unopened and wait until both letters arrived before opening either.

And so, one Saturday morning, nearly two months since the day they first met me, Hazel saw Clara running towards the café, beaming with excitement. She knew it had to be the letter, as she had never seen her friend run once in her life before this.

"I got the letter, but I didn't open it as we promised," she said, slamming the unopened envelope down onto the table where her friend sat.

Hazel opened her purse and pulled out an identical envelope, also still sealed.

"Ready, set, open!"

With bated breath, they tore open the envelopes simultaneously, their eyes scanning the letters eagerly. Clara's hands trembled as she read the contents aloud.

"*Dear Miss Schattinger,*

We are pleased to inform you that your application has been accepted. If you are still interested in taking the position, please prepare for departure to Honolulu within the next month. Detailed instructions will follow. Congratulations, and welcome aboard!"

Hazel's eyes widened with excitement as she read her own letter.

"*If you are still interested in taking the position, please prepare for departure to Honolulu within the next month. Detailed instructions will follow. Congratulations, and welcome aboard*!"

They looked at each other in disbelief, then burst into laughter and tears of joy.

"We did it!" Clara exclaimed. "We're going to Hawaii!"

Hazel hugged her even more tightly than she had the first day they met.

"This is going to be the adventure of a lifetime. I can feel it."

For the next few days, their excitement was more palpable than ever. They filled nearly every hour until their departure, meticulously planning

Chapter 12

out their journey. First, they visited Union Station to inquire about train schedules and fares, learning that a train ride to Los Angeles would have to be their first leg of the trip. They also researched ships sailing from Los Angeles to Honolulu.

"We need to budget carefully," Clara said, making notes in her journal. "Train tickets, ship passage, accommodations... it all adds up." She was so glad that the letter arrived during summer break.

"But it's worth it," Hazel replied, her eyes shining with determination. "This is our dream. We're making it happen."

They continued to meet at the café, discussing every detail of their plans. Clara informed her parents of her decision.

"I'll be careful," Clara assured them. "I've planned everything out and then some."

Hazel, on the other hand, had little to explain to her family.

"Sure, they'll be surprised, but I've always been independent," she said with a shrug.

The days flew by as they prepared for their departure. They packed their trunks with care, selecting clothing and essentials for various occasions. As they had discussed, Clara filled her trunk with her beloved books, paper, and herbal medicine while Hazel packed her sewing kit, dresses, and dancing shoes.

On the day of their departure, they stood on the platform at Union Station, their hearts pounding with anticipation. The train whistle blew, signaling the start of their journey.

"Here we go," Clara said, gripping Hazel's hand.

"To new adventures," Hazel replied, smiling brightly.

As the train pulled out of the station, they looked out the window, watching Denver fade into the distance. Their spirits soared with the promise of new experiences and the thrill of the unknown. They were certain this was the beginning of a new grand adventure, and they were ready to embrace it together.

Clara's Entire List of Books

A Lantern of Love (1921) – A Southern girl's love story sparked by a symbolic lantern. *(Della Campbell MacLeod)*

If Winter Comes (1921) – A misunderstood man finds solace in an unexpected woman. *(Stuart-Menteth)*

Japan and Its Art (1912) – A deep dive into Japan's rich artistic traditions. *(Marcus Bourne Huish)*

John L. Stoddard's Lectures (1897-1898, 1901) – Groundbreaking travelogues with vivid storytelling. *(John Lawson Stoddard)*

Kimono (1921) – A tragic interracial marriage clashes with cultural expectations. *(John Paris)*

Main Street (1920) – A woman fights to modernize a resistant small town. *(Sinclair Lewis)*

Man and Superman (1903) – A witty play exploring power, gender, and ideals. *(George Bernard Shaw)*

Philosophy of Alleyzschel (1879) – Nietzsche's radical views on morality and self-growth. *(Friedrich Wilhelm Nietzsche)*

Pygmalion (1912) – A linguist transforms a flower girl into a lady. *(George Bernard Shaw)*

The Brimming Cup (1921) – A hopeful portrait of small-town Vermont life. *(Dorothy Canfield Fisher)*

The Little Blue Flower (1902) – Short stories filled with wisdom and wonder. *(Henry Van Dyke)*

The Little Minister (1891) – A minister struggles with love and social class. *(J.M. Barrie)*

The Rebirth of Korea (1920) – Korea's awakening to change and independence. *(Hugh Heung-Wo Cynn)*

Unseen Forces (1903) – A woman's visions expose hidden love and deceit. *(S. R. Maxwell)*

Chapter 13

Clara and Hazel disembarked from the ship, their eyes wide with excitement and wonder. They generously tipped the porter handling their trunks, who pasted hotel address labels on their trunks and assured them their luggage would arrive at the hotel room in a few hours.

Clara muttered to herself, "I hope this isn't the last time we see our earthly possessions."

Hazel, meanwhile, was more concerned with trying to hail a taxi.

"Clara, get over here," she called out. "We can't get lost in a place like this."

A taxi pulled up as Clara made her way over to her traveling companion. Hazel swung in and handed the driver their address all in one swift, well-practiced motion, with Clara scooching in beside her. As they pulled away from the curb, the two friends looked at each other, exhaled deeply, and then giggled with a mix of relief and excitement.

"Can you believe we made it this far?" Hazel said, her eyes sparkling with excitement.

Though their employment letter had outlined an itinerary set to start two days from now, they had been advised to arrive early in case of travel delays. While the letter had said they'd be responsible for covering the hotel costs of these two nights, they were more than happy for the opportunity to explore the island.

At every turn of the taxi, Clara was in awe, exclaiming, "Look at that ocean!" or "Do you see that volcanic mountain?" Her joy and excitement were palpable as she soaked in the breathtaking scenery, feeling as though she had fulfilled her lifelong travel dreams within the first hour of their arrival.

In an ironic twist, Hazel felt inclined to be the more practical of the two travelers, reminding Clara to watch how the taxi got to the hotel in case they wanted to come to tour more of the city at some point.

Clara's eyes widened in awe again once the taxi pulled up to the hotel. "Have you ever seen a building this beautiful?" she asked, her voice filled with wonder.

Chapter 13

Hazel smiled.

"This is the Hotel Honolulu, like the letter says."

The next two and a half days passed quickly. After settling into the hotel room they agreed to share, Clara and Hazel quickly found themselves in bed, exhausted by their travels. They spent the following mornings at the beach, basking in the sun and trying out their new swimsuits. The water was warm and inviting, and they reveled in the simple pleasure of swimming in the ocean. In the afternoons, they explored the city, taking a guided walking tour that introduced them to the rich history and vibrant culture of Honolulu. They savored delicious meals at local restaurants, each dish a delightful new experience.

> 1922 Thursday 5, Jan.
> went out swimming with the girls - We were in the water over 1 hr. After ... there went to the

On the second day, detailed letters were delivered to their hotel door. While the letters they'd received in Denver only went as far as directing them to come to the Hotel Honolulu and giving them general recommendations for what to pack, the new letters outlined a much more specific itinerary for them to follow. The new letter laid out what dress code the two were to follow for the next few days and instructed them to report to the executive conference room on the 10th floor each day at 7:30 a.m. starting tomorrow.

Hazel read the letter aloud and commented, "They're going to be surprised to learn how much coffee I need to stay awake at 7:30 a.m."

Clara went to the hotel clerk and requested a wake-up knock on their door.

"Room 967," she told the receptionist, "6:30 a.m. sharp. Thank you."

Though they went to bed early that night, a shared sense of excitement made it hard to sleep. Clara was even more excited as she tossed and turned, even as darkness came over the room, eagerly anticipating the start of their new adventure.

The knock on the door came precisely at 6:30 a.m. as requested, but Clara was already awake, watching the clock, when it came. She smiled and said, "Wake up, Hazel. Our new life is about to begin."

Hazel groaned but got up quickly, thankful that the excitement in Clara's voice was contagious. They dressed quickly, choosing outfits that satisfied the letter's call for 'professional attire' yet still felt comfortable all the same. Clara opted for a tailored navy dress and Hazel a chic gray suit.

As they made their way to the executive conference room, they could feel the energy in the air. Despite the sun was hardly up yet, the hotel was bustling with activity as other new employees also headed to the breakfast meeting. Clara and Hazel exchanged excited glances as they made their way to the executive room.

The conference room was elegantly decorated. Large windows offered a near-panoramic view of the ocean, and a buffet table was set up with an array of pastries, Hawaiian fruits, such as passionfruit, mango, coconuts, papaya, and pineapple, and much to Hazel's relief, plenty of coffee. The two women filled their plates before finding seats at a table near the front.

Shortly after they had taken their seats, a man atop the stage welcomed everyone to the meeting and introduced himself as Daniel, their supervisor. Shortly after greeting everyone warmly, he began the orientation, in which he provided a detailed overview of the company and its responsibilities. Clara listened intently, taking notes and asking questions. Hazel, after finishing her fourth cup of coffee, was also equally engaged.

Daniel went through the itinerary in detail, which included training sessions, team-building activities, and excursions to familiarize them with the cruise ship and its operations. By the end of the session, both Denver girls felt more confident and prepared for the days ahead.

As they left the conference room, Clara turned to Hazel and whispered, "This is going to be an amazing experience. I can feel it."

Hazel nodded, "Absolutely. Let's make the most of it."

They spent the rest of the evening exploring more of Honolulu, savoring the beauty and charm of the city. Each new discovery deepened Clara's appreciation for their surroundings and strengthened her bond with Hazel. As the sun set over the ocean, she knew she would be ready for whatever adventures lay ahead.

The next morning, they were awake, dressed, and well-groomed by 7:15 a.m. Each woman chose an ankle-length dress with a top that exposed very little of their shoulders and arms. Both dresses have defined the waist with a fabric belt or bow.

By the time they entered the executive conference room, about 30 women of various sizes, ages, and backgrounds were seated at different tables. Clara glanced at Hazel with doubt, and seeing her friend's equally perplexed expression only deepened her concern.

Clara led the way to a table with two professionally dressed women about their age. Both were of darker complexion than Clara and Hazel. Both were quite beautiful as well.

"Good morning, I'm Hazel, and this is my friend, Clara. We're from Denver, Colorado. Where are you all from?"

It was immediately obvious that these two beautiful women only spoke a bit of English.

The woman with the longer, straighter hair said only, "Maria from Brazil and friend Gabriela."

Their chat was cut short, however, by a speaker on the podium calling for everyone's attention. In both English and Spanish, he instructed the women to form four groups.

"If you hear your name called, this means you are in Group One. Once you hear your name called, please meet with George, the man in the blue suit, for further instructions. I will call the names starting with Susan Austin, Martha Doberman, Hazel Oldt, Miranda Salinger, and Clara Schattinger."

Hearing their names called, Clara and Hazel proceeded to the door one after the other alongside the other women that now formed Group One. Once the speaker had finished calling out the names of Group One members, George led them down the hall to a smaller room.

"My name is George Wilson," the man in the blue suit affirmed as they walked towards the room, "I am the Director of Guest Services for The Pacific Cruise Company. I will explain the program to you over the next three days once we get settled into our new room. I would like to tell you all that each of you has been selected to serve within our most trusted, most elite group. As members of Group One, you will hold the position

Chapter 13

of being a 'Guest Services Ambassador.' Besides the cruise ship officers, you will be the only set of employees with a private cabin besides the cruise ship officers."

They reached the smaller room after a short walk, which contained chairs and a single conference table. George made a gesture to tell the women to sit where they pleased. Clara and Hazel sat together.

"I encourage questions throughout the presentations," he said, picking up a large set of papers before beginning to walk around the table. "I am handing out a 5-page contract to each of you. Your name and today's date are at the top. You may not leave this room with the contract. Please read it carefully. You must return the signed contracts by 9:00 a.m. If you do not sign the contracts, you will not be allowed to participate in the rest of the seminar, and your room charges will no longer be paid. You may talk among yourselves or ask me questions while reading the contract."

He stopped talking for a moment as he handed the last woman their contract, then, in a softer, less monotonous tone, added,

"Let me say this is a fabulous opportunity to see the world and get paid while doing it. I have been with the company for seven years."

Clara and Hazel each read the contract while drinking another cup of coffee. It explained the position's starting salary, the length of each cruise, how much time they got off between cruises, what their personal expenses looked like, typical cabin size, their clothing allowance, laundry services, and so on and so on. The job description reads, "Guest Service Ambassadors will be tasked with serving the elite guests on each cruise. It will be your job, first and foremost, to fulfill their every request to the best of your ability."

"Did you see the salary?" Clara whispered to Hazel. "That's more than double what I earned as a teacher. Personally, I'm ready to sign this 1-year contract and get my first assignment. What about you?"

Hazel, however, was more cautious about signing the contract.

"I'm still looking for what happens if we want to quit after the first cruise," she told Clara.

"Let's ask George about it," said Clara as she raised her hand. Hazel began to shake her head at this idea, but was too late to discourage Clara from getting George's attention.

Once George came over, Clara asked, "What happens if I want to quit after the first cruise?"

"If you look on page 5, you'll see the contract states that you'll be paid $40 once the first cruise ends. You can opt-out after that, but if you're not based in Hawaii, you must pay for your travel expenses back to Hawaii or your point of origin. If you choose to continue, the next opportunity to leave the position is after each 6-month assignment."

"OK, another question." Clara continued. "When will we get our first assignment?"

"This afternoon, if you sign your contract by nine, of course," George said with a smile.

As soon as George left the two girls to answer another question across the table, Clara immediately signed the contract. She told herself it would be fun, even if they quit after the first cruise. Hazel took a bit longer, checking over the fine print some more to make sure George was telling the full truth but eventually decided to sign the contract too, after a bad caffeine headache made reading too much to handle. They handed in their contracts and took a brief walk outside until 9:00 a.m.

The morning was spent listening to George's detailed presentation about their roles, responsibilities, and the various aspects of the job. He covered everything from the etiquette expected of them to the types of requests they might encounter. Clara paid close attention, taking notes and occasionally exchanging glances of amazement and anticipation with Hazel, who was more concerned with fighting off her growing fatigue than the presentation before them. Still, she nodded and smiled at Clara when she caught her friend's glance, eager for the day when they could finally put this presentation's information to use together.

Once they finished listening to George's presentation, everyone in Group 1 ate a light lunch of a meat dish with two scoops of steamed white rice courtesy of the hotel before gathering back in the conference room for their assignments.

After lunch, George informed them about their assignment by saying, "Clara and Hazel, you have both been assigned to the Tokyo cruise. It will be 21 days long, so please begin to pack accordingly."

Chapter 13

Clara's face reflected pure excitement, while Hazel's had a touch of apprehension in her eyes.

"Tokyo's a bit far, isn't it?" Hazel asked her friend, unsure of how far is a bit far.

"Almost as far from the U.S. as you can get by boat," Clara answered, "and all the better if you ask me!"

After their 4:30 p.m. dismissal, Clara and Hazel rushed to their room to change into swimsuits. Somehow, despite its proximity, the two women had been to about everywhere, but they decided an one more trip to the beach.

A quick walk brought Clara and Hazel to the beach, which was alive with activity, from surfers riding the high tide to sunbathing in the rays. They joined in, enjoying both the water and the sun in turn. After an hour of fun, they bought some sandwiches and drinks, then found a quiet spot on the beach to eat, savoring the sunset's color and the peaceful ambiance.

Later in the night, back in their hotel room, Clara worked on sewing a silk camisole for Hazel while Hazel read aloud from *Unseen Forces* by S.R. Maxwell, a love story about a woman who can see the future. The soothing rhythm of Hazel's voice and the calm of the evening enveloped Clara in a layer of deep tranquility.

Before bed, Clara wrote in her diary, reflecting on the pair's exciting yet uncertain new future. In her entry, she expressed her gratitude to Hazel for their friendship, which began at a Denver café and had profoundly changed her life.

But as long as we're together, Clara wrote in the last sentence of her entry, *I know we'll be fine.*

Happily, worn out by the many events of their long day together, Clara thought of how lucky she had been to have found such a true friend by what seemed to her sheer coincidence. Her reflections were brief, however, as she soon drifted off into sleep much more easily than in previous nights, the sound of the waves echoing in her mind.

The training sessions on cruise ship etiquette began early at 6:30 a.m. The day included a presentation by a female nurse on managing menstrual cycles on board. The clinic supplied necessary menstrual products and required women to check in at the start of their cycle. Missing two cycles prompted a pelvic exam, and suspected pregnancies resulted in employment termination at the next port.

A private health check followed, where the nurse recorded menstrual cycle details and medical conditions. Hazel noted to Clara how a couple of women were discreetly removed and not seen again.

The afternoon was spent fitting uniforms: a light gray wool skirt, navy blue jacket, white silk blouse, navy and green scarf, and navy-blue stacked heels. They also received lace panties, garter belts, camisoles, and silk stockings, with two complete uniforms delivered to their rooms.

The next morning picked up where the previous session had left off, with the nurse giving a stern talk on sexual health before explaining condom use, describing the symptoms of sexually transmitted diseases, and highlighting the importance of self-protection. The session concluded by covering the protocol for dealing with the Spanish flu, in which the nurse emphasized the importance of mask-wearing, quarantine procedures, and symptom management.

The evening before their first cruise, Clara and Hazel celebrated with a fancy dinner and a show featuring a mind reader. Returning to their hotel, Clara received several forwarded letters. Among them was a heartbreaking letter from her childhood friend Hoki, who was dying from the pandemic flu. Clara, overwhelmed with sadness, wrote a letter to her parents before bed, knowing she couldn't reply to Hoki in time.

The next morning, they found two large cardboard boxes at their door. Inside both were sets of the same uniforms, which they were thrilled to see fit perfectly after trying them on. With anticipation, they tried on the perfectly fitting uniforms. While Clara braided and twisted her hair, Hazel twirled in front of the mirror, smiling.

"You're gonna wear that thing out before we even hit the boat! Clara said with a laugh.

Their final training session ended with an elegant lunch and was filled with emotional farewells. The women, having bonded over the past few days, discussed their ship assignments and discovered they would be with three familiar faces and many more would be without.

After packing their belongings and packing luggage tags, Clara and Hazel joined the three other women for dinner. They reflected on the whirlwind week they had before each guessing

Chapter 13

over cocktails what their future together would be like.

The next morning, Clara and Hazel woke up early, filled with both excitement and nervous energy. Each dressed in their uniforms and double-checked their luggage to make sure everything was perfect for their departure.

When Hazel opened the door to put her truck in the hallway, she noticed an envelope on the floor sliding into their room. 'HAZEL OLDT' was handwritten in large capital letters on the front of the envelope. Hazel felt a chill go down her spine.

"Clara, look what was in the hallway?" Hazel said once she mustered up the strength to return to her bed. Clara turned around from her suitcase and looked at the envelope. "What do you suppose it is?"

"With your luck, probably some kind of promotion," her friend joked. Hazel only shook her in response.

"I am afraid to open it. Do you think you can open it for me?"

Clara nonchalantly swiped the envelope away from Hazel's outstretched hand and opened it as though it was a piece of junk mail. She almost thought of reading the letter herself for the sake of her roommate, too, but some instinct warned her against it at the last moment, so she passed the letter back to Hazel, who was nearly shaking when she took back the letter.

Hazel almost immediately burst into tears.

"San Francisco?! Clara, they changed my assignment!" she said in such loud astonishment someone three floors up could've heard her crystal clear. She read over the rest of the letter and then looked up into the somber eyes of her friend. "I leave tomorrow on the Ruby Princess. We won't be together."

Clara was stunned at the news, but she also realized that she needed to be leaving in the next five minutes to be on time for her destination. She tried to console Hazel as quickly as time permitted, who had since been left speechless by the news, staring absently at the single piece of paper that had torn her away from all the futures she'd been planning out the past week.

"Good luck, Hazel," Clara said, giving her friend a tight hug. "I know you'll do great."

"You too, Clara," Hazel replied, hugging her back. Then, with a strength that impressed Clara,

Hazel brushed away her tears and smiled at her friend. "Hey, at least we'll have a ton of stories to share when we see each other again."

Clara gave Hazel one last hug and said,

"Hazel, you really have changed my life forever. I can't thank you enough for what you've done." She withdrew from their embrace and made her way over to the door.

"Write when you have time," she said to her friend in her final farewell. "Have a wonderful trip, and remember, I will always love you!"

Tears had once again begun streaming down Hazel's cheeks, and it was through stifled sob that she called out, "Of course I'll write! I love you too, Clara! And you be safe out there, okay?"

With one last smile, Hazel placed her trunk into the hallway and closed the door behind her. The unexpected farewell had set her behind schedule, and so it was in a state of nearly complete physical exhaustion that she saluted the captain and made her way on board the cruise ship. She had been forced to jog well over a quarter mile in the summer Hawaii sun to arrive on time, all while carrying her trunk no less.

But it was with a deep breath of determination and excitement that Hazel found her way to the Guest Services Ambassador quarters. The start of a new chapter in her life had finally begun, and Hazel was ready to make the most of it.

Clara was left standing in the doorway with tears streaming down her cheeks, "I will write. Best wishes to you, friend."

With one last smile, Clara went back into the hotel room for one last night, but this time she was alone. placed her trunk in the hallway. Later in the day, she left the hotel and walked down the sidewalk to view the ship that she would board tomorrow afternoon. Clara was ready to embrace the adventures and challenges that lay ahead. This was the start of a new chapter in her life, and she was ready to make the most of it.

Chapter 14

Clara woke up early the next day in a quiet room, restless with anticipation and anxiety about setting sail that afternoon. She got up, splashed cold water on her face, and brewed a pot of tea. Seeking solace, she turned to her diary.

"I have no idea what's in store for me," she wrote. *"What if I end up hating this job?"*

Once her diary could offer no more relief, Clara put it away and began rearranging her trunk once more. With her new uniform in mind, she stacked the rest of her clothes as the first layer. She marveled at the array of silk lingerie she now owned, a luxury she had never indulged in before.

"What would Mom and Dad think," she said aloud to herself. Hearing her own voice aloud was a novelty. When was the last time she said something aloud to herself? She interpreted it all as a sign of her growing unease, then decided to take a bath to calm her nerves.

Taking a deep breath and a final glance in the mirror, Clara tried to bolster her resolve. "I can do this," she thought to herself. She had put on her uniform. She had done her makeup impeccably, styled her hair, taken her time to work it into a neat French twist, and filed her nails down to as acceptable length as she could get. She had done everything there was to do and then some.

After checking out at the front desk, Clara stepped outside and began retracing her steps from the day before. And, sure enough, there it was, looming ahead-the cruise ship that would be her home for the foreseeable future. With a mixture of trepidation and determination, Clara continued towards it unflinchingly.

She slipped on her jacket, adjusting her name badge as she did so, and mustered up the smile she planned to greet cruise guests with as she exited the room.

At the end of the ramp, a distinguished gentleman greeted her.

"Good afternoon," he said, pausing to look at her nametag, "Miss Clara Schattinger, Guest Ambassador. Welcome to Pacific Cruise Corporation! I'm Daniel, the Cruise Director. We are delighted that you've joined our team. Omar here will assist you in finding the Grand Ballroom and your cabin." He gestured to the larger buffer man standing beside him, who was wearing a much less distinguished outfit. "We're convening at 2:30 for a Welcome Reception in the Grand Ballroom. Please head over there once you've settled into your room – and make sure you're in uniform," he added. "Once again, welcome aboard!"

"Thank you," Clara replied with nervous enthusiasm. "I'm thrilled to be a part of the team. Looking forward to meeting everyone."

Omar silently grabbed Clara's luggage away from her before turning back into the cruise ship's innards. Clara followed closely behind him. He stopped in front of a room only a few levels below the deck, which caught Clara off-guard since she had expected to be placed in a room well below the water level. She almost said something but decided against it at the last second.

As he opened the door, Clara's eyes widened in awe. "Oh, it's beautiful—no, glamorous," she said, taken aback. "Are you certain this is the right room?"

Omar nodded affirmatively. "Yes, this is your assigned cabin." He dropped her luggage off

Chapter 14

beside the front door. And with that, he left as silently as he came.

During the reception, Clara found herself surrounded by a sea of new faces, tasked with the challenge of meeting nearly a hundred new employees. After a whirlwind of names and faces, she was certain she'd forget within the hour, Clara was grateful to see Helen, Ruth, and Anna, three of the women she had bonded with during training, clumped together in the corner of the room. Though they could only talk briefly, Clara arranged to meet them in her cabin #520 before the 6:00 p.m. dinner.

Retreating to her cabin as soon as she saw the opportunity, Clara shed her uniform in favor of a cozy bathrobe, set her alarm for 5:00 p.m., and collapsed onto the bed. Exhaustion quickly overtook her, and she felt she'd only closed her eyes for a minute or two. The shrill ring of her alarm jolted her back awake. She freshened her makeup and slipped into a suitable dress for the evening ahead.

At a knock on her door, Clara called out, "Come in. I'll be ready in a minute." She was trying to squeeze into a pair of too tight shoes now. The door swung open, all three of her friends from behind it.

"How did you find the reception?" she asked them as they filed into her room.

Anna, the tallest of the group, spoke up first. "I still have so many questions," she admitted.

Helen, who Clara always remembered for her stunning auburn hair, chimed in.

"I think I've managed to figure out a few things, but I'm still in the dark about a lot of stuff, too. Like, when do we get our first paycheck? And if it's a check, can we cash it on the boat, or do we have to wait until we're back home? There are so many things I didn't think of before that now seem so important."

"I'm taking it one day at a time," interjected Ruth, the most laid-back of the three. "Right now, all I want is some food and alcohol. Let's get going."

Grabbing her keys, Clara followed the women out into the hallway, where they soon saw Omar passing by. Ruth was the first to call out to him.

Chapter 14

"Hey Omar, where can a lady get some food and alcohol around here?" All four of the girls laughed.

"Follow me, ladies," Omar replied in his matter-of-fact manner. He led them toward the employee bar and cafeteria on the third level. "Remember, you mustn't be seen by the guests when you're out of uniform. Use the employee elevator when you can. If that's not an option, take the stairs. Also, keep in mind that the cost of food and alcohol will be deducted from your paycheck. But don't worry; you'll pick up tips and tricks along the way. Most of us purchase alcohol and dry goods when the ship stops at various ports of call. We are allowed to store such items in our cabins. I'm sure you'll catch on quickly, but still, feel free to ask me anything."

The frankness of his speech caught Clara off-guard. She had expected more of the reservedness she saw in their first meeting when Ruth called out to Omar.

"This might be our go-to guy," thought Clara.

Seated at a table, they ordered a variety of alcohol. Clara ordered two shots of bourbon straight-up, while Ruth ordered a Manhattan over ice, Anna had a glass of Merlot, and Helen had vodka and soda. The drinks ignited a lively conversation.

"Are our cabins next to each other? Mine's number 405."

"I'm in 504."

"414."

"Mine's 520," Clara remarked.

"Yeah, we know, Clara. We were just there, weren't we?" said Ruth jokingly. The other two women laughed while Clara blushed and tried to smile.

"It makes no sense," Anna said once she'd quit laughing. "Why are we scattered across two levels? We should try to remember each other's numbers for easier meetups," Anna suggested.

"Passengers start boarding tomorrow at 11:00 a.m. What should we do then? I hope they don't ask us for directions. I have no clue where anything is," Helen said.

"Let's stand around in our new uniforms and look like pretty mannequins. That's my plan," Ruth quipped, lighting another cigarette.

Chapter 14

Their conversation continued for an hour or so. Then, at Clara's suggestion, they ordered dinner. The food, while not exceptional, was satisfying enough for their first meal together.

"I'm exhausted. They mentioned the time we need to be in the Grand Ballroom at the reception, but I can't recall it now. Does anyone remember?" Clara inquired.

"Drank that much already?" Ruth joked.

"I thought I heard them say eight a.m.," Anna answered. "And they said we'd receive tomorrow's itinerary outside our cabin door tonight, right?"

"They had better include a tour of this massive ship, too, so we can answer any questions the guests might have. Otherwise, I'll be directing every guest to Omar."

Ruth yawned and said, "It is getting late, and I need my beauty sleep."

Anna stood up, "It is later than I thought."

"Goodnight, everyone," Clara said as they dispersed.

Back in her cabin, Clara picked up the itinerary left by the door and began to read it as she set out her things for the next day.

"Tomorrow doesn't look too exciting. So much to learn. At least the tour is first on the list," she thought as she slipped back into her robe and set her alarm. Exhaustion and the drinks helped her to drift off to sleep within minutes.

The next morning, Clara rose around seven. The night before, Helen had suggested getting up early to beat the breakfast rush in the employee cafeteria, and sure enough, Clara saw Helen and Ann in line together as soon as she was through the cafeteria doors. The three of them sat together, eating and drinking coffee in relative silence until Ruth finally made her way to the cafeteria ten or so minutes after they'd sat down.

"It's easy to identify the different levels of employees by their uniforms," Clara noted once Ruth had joined the three of them. She discreetly pointed out a group of sharply dressed men who had entered the room to prove her point.

"Where have they been hiding those good-looking men?' Ruth said with a grin. "I hope we get to work closely with them today."

"They don't seem as lost as most of us here," Clara noted.

Chapter 14

Before she could finish her thought, Ann was already heading over to introduce herself and her friends to the men. While the move caught the other three women off-guard, they soon followed their friend, and in no time, both groups had gathered around a table, sharing introductions.

"I guess you could say we're the male version of your positions – with three years of experience, that is," a man who had introduced himself as Steve Evans said with a touch of pride. "Feel free to ask us anything. We're not tied to the captain or any officers."

"Oh, would you look at the time? It's nearly eight already," Helen said, gesturing to her watch. "We should head to the Grand Ballroom. It's around 9:00 a.m. We don't want to be late on our first day."

The men all grinned, and a man named Roger spoke up.

"We're the cream of the employee crop. Couldn't you tell that by the rooms they gave us? Not everyone gets rooms like that, let me tell you. They won't kick off until we're there."

"Trust us," Steve said. "You can unwind. They rely on us more than you realize. Keep that in mind."

So, they sat together in the cafeteria for a while longer, everyone making idle chit-chat except for Helen, who nervously fidgeted about in her chair.

When they did finally leave, one of the men led them through a shortcut via the side entrance to the Grand Ballroom.

"Front row seats reserved for the nine of us, ladies," he pointed out as they made their way into the room. A speaker came onto the stage almost immediately after they had filed into their seats.

The opening talk was brief for the front row. Even though the ballroom was packed with new employees, the nine Guest Ambassadors were whisked away after the welcome address to another private training session. Since the men had three years of experience, they led the session along with Daniel, the Cruise Director.

The training session was intense but informative. Daniel covered everything from emergency procedures to guest interaction protocols while the experienced male ambassadors shared practical tips they had learned over the years. Clara took copious notes, feeling more prepared with each passing minute.

By the time the session ended, Clara felt a mix of exhaustion and exhilaration. She knew the coming days would be challenging, but she was ready to embrace her new role with confidence.

As she made her way back to her cabin, she reflected on the whirlwind of events that had brought her to this point. She was determined to succeed, no matter what challenges lay ahead. With a renewed sense of purpose, she prepared for the rest of her journey, ready to face whatever the cruise had in store for her.

"Hello and good morning, all," said Daniel, standing in front of his chair at the table. It was now afternoon: time for the formal introductions between staff members. Ruth had told Daniel they had all met each other before, during coffee, but he insisted on having the introductions, nonetheless. And so, here they were. "I met you briefly yesterday, but today, we will get into the details of your positions. First, I am your supervisor for the duration of this 21-day cruise. Your entire job is based on making the first-class guests to be always happy. Please remember that many of these guests are used to having staff at home. Your jobs will be to serve as stand-ins for this staff on the cruise."

He cleared his throat and then continued.

"All requests within reason will be considered mandatory for you to fulfill. Come to me with any questions, but if I am not available, please ask the five gentlemen sitting near you. They have years of experience. However, and trust me when I say this, each cruise has its share of unique problems and solutions. You will learn fast and, I hope, laugh frequently. Now, then, let's go around the room and get to know each other. Ladies, please say your name, introduce yourself, tell us why you decided to join Pacific Cruise Corporation and ask one question you have about the cruise. The gentlemen will say their name and, to illustrate what I was saying before, tell the unique situation that they have encountered on a cruise."

"We're not actually doing that, are we?" one of the men cried out. Daniel ignored this.

"Let begin with Ruth," he said before ceding the floor.

"Hi, my name is Ruth. I was named after my grandmother, who died before I was born. I'm from Chicago. If you have ever been there, you'll know why I wanted this opportunity." A few of the men laughed. "I have a college degree in business from the University of Illinois. I am the oldest of four children. I want to explore the world and am still deciding whether I want a cruise ship career that's maybe more on the business side of things – but I'm still glad to be here all the same, beginning with the hospitality side. My question is: Do we get assigned to a certain number of guests located close together?"

Daniel replied, "Yes, each Guest Ambassador gets assigned approximately 10 cabins or about the same number of guests. All the assigned guests are first-class passengers. I cannot emphasize enough that you fulfill their requests in a timely manner. It could be delivering fresh flowers or ice, ordering transportation for their shore excursions, etc. If they ask, you will provide for all their requests."

Steve stood up to show he wanted to go next.

"Hey there, I'm Steve, and I hail from Omaha, Nebraska. Let me tell you about a wild ride I had on my first cruise. Picture this: three classy, wealthy ladies in the fanciest cabin with three bedrooms. They'd order room service for every meal, and guess who they asked to deliver it? Yours truly. Now, here's the kicker. Every time I showed up, they'd have the door slightly ajar. I'd knock, they'd say, 'Come in,' and bam! There they were, lounging in open bathrobes, completely in the buff. I'd set their meal down, they'd nod thanks, and that was it. Not a single word exchanged beyond 'thank you.' Housekeeping would clear out the used dishes, and the cycle continued. Now, let's hear if anyone's got a story to top that!" He finished with a mischievous grin.

"Hey folks, I'm Roger, representing Ohio. Now, I might not outdo Steve's tale, but here's one for the books. I once had this elderly couple who practically made cruise ships their permanent address. They'd been sailing the seas for years, apparently, and would only emerge for dinner. Oh, and they always had to have a balcony, too. Now, here's where it gets interesting. Every few nights, they'd order top-shelf cognac, even though the bottles I delivered from before would still be nearly full. I knew this because they'd give 'em to me and throw them out whenever I brought them a new one. And just like Steve's ladies, this couple had a dress code of sorts—him in his briefs, her in silk panties."

"But here's the twist. Towards the end of the cruise, after knocking back more than a few bottles of cognac, fully emptied, the housekeeping staff made a grim discovery: the couple, stark naked and tragically deceased in their bed. The ship's doctor pinned it on alcohol poisoning. Now, that's a story you don't hear every day." Roger concluded with a solemn nod, acknowledging the weight of the narrative.

No one volunteered too quickly after that story, and so Clara felt obliged to take this opportunity to introduce herself and get it over with.

"Hello, my name is Clara, from Denver, Colorado. I taught school for a few years, but it wasn't too exciting. I applied for the job because I've always wanted to travel the world. My three siblings are married with children. That was not what I wanted for my life, so here I am. My question: Do we ever get any days off while the ship is at sea?"

Daniel replied, "You get 10 hours off at each port. You can go sightseeing, shopping, or stay on board and sleep. If you have demanding guests, you will have to be ready to work 18 hours a day for several days. You are guaranteed 6 hours off each day along with time to eat and shower."

"Thank you for the answer to my question," Clara said. She was glad to be done with her introduction.

"Hey everyone, I'm George, the short guy from Hawaii. My story might not be as wild as the ones you've heard, but here goes. On our last cruise, I arranged a private driver for a lovely middle-aged couple from California. We were docked in Nagoya, Japan, and they had their hearts set on dining at a specific hotel restaurant. But there ended up being a bit of a mix-up with the timing, and they ended up cutting it way too close to the ship's departure."

"Long story short, they almost missed the boat. And when I say almost missed the boat, I really do mean *almost* missed the boat. I'd never seen anyone cut it as close as they did. It was only thanks to some quick thinking and sending another driver to fetch them from the hotel that we avoided a major disaster. The story ended happily, but let me tell you, I was sweating bullets the whole time." George finished with a relieved chuckle, glad that everything turned out alright in the end.

"I'll go next. Hi, I'm Ann, and I'm from California. My parents thought it was good to move west during the Gold Rush. That was a bust, but mom got pregnant while they were there and so here I am. I'm not sure that I want to see the world as much as everyone else here, but I do know that I wanted to get out of California. My question is, why do the women need to deal with the same weird things as the gentlemen?"

Daniel jumped in to say, "Anna, that is an excellent question, but I do not have an answer. The group of women that you trained with in Hawaii was the first group of women ever hired by this cruise corporation. The women were divided across three cruise ships. Since this cruise is the only 21-day trip, the four women were the most fit applicants for the job out of the training class."

Anna replied, "Oh, thank you for being candid."

"Probably means we were the smartest," Clara whispered to Ruth.

"Or the best looking," Ruth whispered back. Clara let out a suppressed chuckle, but thankfully, Daniel didn't seem to notice. Another man began to introduce himself.

"Hi, my name is Carlos. I am from Texas. And yes, I speak English and Spanish. My unique story is not funny, but it shows that even though guests are often annoying, we must still serve them with kindness and respect. So, one time, on a cruise I was working on, there were these two young women who were traveling together. I could tell that they had been wealthy their entire life by their clothes and their walk, you know. They were pretty normal for the first day or so, but then, for whatever reason, they began asking me all their questions in Spanish. They knew very little Spanish, but they were trying to impress me or play a game with me or something I still don't know. Their questions were difficult to understand – they were both pretty bad speakers – and that continued on the entire rest of the trip. I would answer in English because they did not understand enough Spanish to actually hold a conversation in it, but then, sometimes, they'd get mad at me for answering in English. Sometimes, they even pretended they only spoke Spanish, even though we had talked to each other in English a couple of times at the very beginning of the trip. All I can say is that it was not a very fun trip."

"Hey there, I'm Helen, hailing from the Big Apple. Former ballet dancer here, seeking a change of pace and hoping for some fun on the high seas. As I've gotten older, dancing slowly started to offer me less of the excitement I craved, so here I am, ready to shake things up. Now, onto my query: When's the earliest I'll need to be up and ready to cater to my assigned guests? I'm not exactly thrilled about early mornings."

"Helen, it really depends on your guests' preferences," David said in a stiff manner. "Some might want breakfast served by you as early as 6:00 a.m., while others might be fine with kitchen servers handling it. It's all about the guests' wishes. And remember, your job is to fulfill whatever those wishes may be, no matter the time."

"Hey folks, I'm Sean, coming at you from the D.C. area. Former federal government drone here, but let me tell you, sitting at a desk day in and day out? It's not my jam. One thing's for sure about life on a cruise ship—you'll never be bored. But tired? Yeah, that's a given.

"Now, onto my story. Picture this: two dudes in adjoining rooms, claiming to be old high school buddies. But let's say I had my suspicions that they were more than pals. One morning, I'm delivering breakfast at 9:00 a.m. to one room, as requested. When the door opens, it's clear one of them is still in bed, and it looked like they'd spent the night together."

Daniel interjected to provide context to Sean's narrative, "Let me clarify something here. There are no rules about who can have a relationship with whom, especially within the privacy of their own cabins. Our job is simple: provide the services requested, no judgment necessary."

Sean nodded and continued, "Exactly. Our role is to ensure every guest has an enjoyable experience, regardless of their personal life. Love is love and all that."

The introductions continued around the room, each new Guest Ambassador sharing their unique background and aspirations while the experienced gentlemen shared more of the fascinating and sometimes bizarre experiences they'd had to work on other cruises.

As the meeting wrapped up, Daniel stood and addressed the group.

"Thank you all for sharing. It's important we understand and support each other as a team. Now, let's move on to the practical part of your training. We'll start with a tour of the ship to familiarize you with all key areas you'll need to know to assist our first-class guests effectively."

Chapter 15

As the first weeks unfolded, the women delved into every aspect of their intricate job, mastering the intricacies of the ship's layout along with the finer details of their duties. They formed close bonds with their male counterparts, often sharing meals as a cohesive team.

Clara and Steve naturally emerged as the unofficial leaders of the Guest Ambassadors team. Drawing on her previous experience as a teacher, Clara showcased exceptional leadership skills, while Steve proved to be an invaluable collaborator. Together, they listened to suggestions, brainstormed solutions, and strategized options to present to the administration.

At the end of the second week, Captain McAllister and his officers graciously hosted a formal dinner for the Guest Ambassadors in his opulent suite. Wanting all members to attend, the dining staff covered any guest requests for a two-hour period unless it was an emergency. Though technically off-duty for the occasion, the ambassadors remained in uniform, ready to assist their assigned guests in case of an emergency.

The dinner commenced promptly at 8:00 p.m., with the Captain's Maître d' expertly seating officers and guests at the oval table to encourage lively conversation. Positioned midway along the long side of the table, Captain McAllister was flanked by Clara on his left and, luckily, Steve on her left. The highest-ranking officer sat to the captain's right, with Helen seated next to them. Notably, none of the women were seated adjacent to each other, outnumbered as they were by their male colleagues.

As the dinner progressed, Clara found herself at the center of the Captain's attention, his focus directed mostly towards her. Initially feeling self-conscious, she soon realized that her seating arrangement had been intentional. Despite her attempts to engage with Steve, he was engrossed in conversation with the officer seated to his left, leaving Clara to field the Captain's inquiries on her own.

Glancing around the table, Clara observed everyone immersed in conversation, thoroughly enjoying the sumptuous four-course meal with perfectly paired wines. With two options for each course, Clara carefully selected dishes that were easy to eat, ensuring no risk of spillage or embarrassment.

As the conversation continued and the Captain's questions persisted, Clara found herself silently wishing for an emergency with one of her assigned guests, longing for a graceful exit from the intense scrutiny. However, her wishes remained unfulfilled, and she endured the exchange until the last drop of after-dinner wine had been savored.

As the dinner ended, Captain McAllister graciously stood at the door, bidding farewell to each ambassador with a handshake. Positioning herself among her friends, Clara tactfully avoided getting caught in a one-on-one conversation with the captain. Meanwhile, the officers remained behind in the dining room, engrossed in their own discussions.

As the ambassador team gathered in the closed employee cafeteria for some debriefing of the dinner, Steve initiated the conversation, acknowledging the significance of the evening.

"Just so the ladies know that dinner was the first time the guys have been invited to the captain's table. Thanks for adding some estrogen to this cruise. We gained some status with the captain because of you ladies. The food and wine were excellent," Steve remarked, appreciating the company of the female ambassadors.

Roger expressed concern for Clara, inquiring about her experience with her dinner partner. "Clara, how did you survive your dinner partner's conversation?" he asked.

Steve chimed in, acknowledging Clara's efforts. "Don't think that I did not notice, Clara. You know that I tried to say something twice," he admitted.

Helen empathized with Clara, acknowledging the challenge she faced. "I felt sorry for you. He had you trapped," she sympathized.

Anna voiced her curiosity, wanting to know more about Clara's encounter. "Was he at least interesting? Let's give Clara a chance to talk," she suggested.

Clara recounted her experience, expressing her relief that the dinner had concluded. "That was intense. I wished that one of my guests would have an emergency so I could leave, but that never happened. I hope it was a one-and-done dinner, although the food and wine were amazing," she reflected.

The conversation continued for another hour, with Clara expressing her gratitude to the team for their support and camaraderie. "Before we go to bed, I want to thank this team for recognizing my place next to the boss. We need to continue to support each other for the rest of this cruise. I am exhausted, so I am leaving," she concluded before bidding goodnight to her colleagues.

As Helen, Ruth, and Anna walked back to their cabins, Helen made a curious observation. "Am I the only one who noticed that the captain's left hand was never seen on the table?" she remarked.

Anna mumbled, "What a bastard!"

Ruth agreed, acknowledging the potential discomfort Clara may have felt. "We need to support Clara. I don't think that we should tell her that we noticed his absent left hand. If she wants to talk, she will tell us. Let's drop the subject," she suggested.

Helen pondered the implications further. "What if she liked it? We can see how she looks at Steve. I think they have something going on besides leadership," she mused, hinting at a potential romantic connection between Clara and Steve.

As the days passed in the Pacific, the topic of the captain's dinner was never mentioned again, but it lingered in the back of everyone's minds. Meanwhile, Daniel, the Cruise Director, planned a grand party for all the guests to celebrate as the ship crossed the International Dateline in the mid-Pacific Ocean, marking 180 degrees' longitude.

> 24
> Jan. Tuesday 24, 1922 '23
> Wed. July 11-'23
> We crossed the international date line and skipped a day to-day. Wrote letters on deck this a.m. - Refused to go on deck with the girls

While the female ambassadors continued to collect their own unique stories from their assigned guests, an unexpected and somber tale emerged from Helen.

Helen's first story involved the tragic death of one of her guests. He was traveling back to India to be with his family after the recent passing of his wife. Having moved to the United States many years ago, they had built a life together in California, raising four children. However, with their children having returned to India to reconnect with family, the man embarked on this cruise alone to return to his homeland.

Tragically, he passed away alone in his cabin, and Helen discovered him after he failed to respond to a knock on the door. With solemn reverence, the gentleman was prepared for burial at sea in a small room above the deck. Deckhands carefully sewed him into a canvas bag, surrounding him with flowers and fruit. Weighted with sandbags, he was placed on a board and covered with a British flag.

As the ship's officers and Guest Ambassadors gathered around the body to offer support to Helen, a priest read the services. With a respectful ceremony, the board was raised, and the body gently slid off into the vast expanse of the sea, marking his final journey home. It was a poignant reminder of the fragility of life amidst the vastness of the ocean.

After days at sea, the ship finally docked at Yokohama Port. Clara, Helen, Ruth, Anna, and Steve wasted no time in disembarking, eager to make the most of their time on land, relishing the freedom of being out of their uniforms. Along the waterfront, they found numerous shop stalls offering handmade souvenirs for tourists. However, Steve, being familiar with the port, steered the group away from the touristy shopping stalls and hailed a taxi to take them downtown to a specific shopping district.

In the bustling streets of downtown Yokohama, they indulged in shopping, tasting delicious street food, and admiring the unique clothing worn by the locals. Many men sported long hair pinned up on the top of their heads with a nail, along with long, baggy bloomer trousers and vests made from grass linen.

After their shopping spree, Steve arranged for a rickshaw ride to take them to the hillside surrounded by cryptomeria trees, where they visited several stunning temples adorned with colorful designs and intricate carvings. At one temple, the guide instructed them to clap their hands, and they were amazed to hear the dragon's growl echo in response.

At another temple, they marveled at the 140 dragons encircling the area, each slightly different from the others. They were particularly intrigued by the inverted dragon, believed to guard the temple against misfortune.

They also had the opportunity to tour a small museum housing the famous sleeping cat, believed to be the manifestation of the Buddha of Healing, along with the original sculptures of Hear No Evil, See No Evil, and Speak No Evil.

As the day ended, Steve ensured they wouldn't be late getting back to the ship by arranging for a taxi. Looking forward to their next adventure, he mentioned their plan to visit the Imperial Theater and Museum the following day.

Helen jokingly suggested, "Steve should consider resigning from his position on the ship to become a travel guide for American tourists in Japan, impressed by his knowledge and expertise."

However, Steve modestly replied, "I don't know enough Japanese to become a tour guide."

The following day began early, with Steve arranging a taxi for their trip to the Imperial

Theater and Museum. Their driver surprised them with excellent English skills, explaining that he had studied the language in night school for three years. He expressed his ambition to visit New York City, prompting Clara to reassure him that they wouldn't mind him traveling to their country, as it mirrored their own journey to his homeland.

During their excursion, they marveled at numerous temples, some ancient and one boasting an impressive 10,000 statues, each adorned with multiple hands. They also toured the Imperial Museum, and as they traversed the streets, they witnessed preparations for a holy day, observing the gods of Utsava Murti being carried out in palanquins and returning at sunset.

Their driver proved to be an asset, as Helen requested a stop at a bank to exchange currency. The driver willingly obliged, dropping them off at the bank and patiently waiting nearby until they returned, ensuring their safety and convenience.

Continuing their journey, they visited an elegant jewelry factory, where they observed artisans crafting delicate cloisonné glass vases adorned with layers of gold borders and painted enamel. Clara couldn't resist purchasing two vases and a necklace, while the other women refrained due to limited disposable cash.

With minutes to spare, they rushed back to the ship, changed into their uniforms, and returned to duty as the ship prepared to depart for its next destination: Seoul, Korea. As the engines started and the ship began to back out, they eagerly anticipated the adventures that awaited them in their next port of call.

SAMPLE OF RECEIPTS FROM AUNT CLARA'S DIARY

$1 IN 1922 = $18.79 IN 2025

Saturday, December 9, 1922	1922	2025
Ticket to Yokohama by ship	$118.00	$2,217.22
Drayage	.75	14.09
Tips	5.00	93.95
Beads for me	2.00	37.58
Beads for Mrs. B.	2.50	46.98
Box	.25	4.70
Rickshaw	.75	14.09
Pictures	.15	2.81
Kamasutra	.50	9.40
Pictures	8.00	150.32
Lantern	.65	12.21
Pearl beads	5.00	93.95
Peking street food	1.00	18.70
Mailing Mrs. B's box	.17	3.19
Box for pearls	.50	9.40
Rickshaw	.40	7.52
Tip	.25	4.70
Tickets to Nikko	1.27	23.86
Cider and lunch	.20	3.76
Temple tickets	.45	8.45
Peaches	.25	4.70
Ticket to Tokyo	1.07	20.11
Room in Nikko	5.00	93.95
Room in Tokyo	1.90	35.70
Meals in Tokyo	2.25	42.27
Picture in Nikko	.75	14.09
Tips	.30	5.64
Pen	1.50	28.19
Hotel Belmont	3.75	70.46
Trunk storage at wharf	2.90	54.49
Tickets to Kyoto	2.80	52.61
Street car	.20	3.76

Chapter 16

With the Guest Ambassadors becoming familiar with their guests' preferences, they managed to gather as a group most days, relishing the opportunity to share a bottle of wine in one of their cabins.

It was after one of these meetings when, upon returning to her suite, Clara noticed a sealed envelope placed neatly on her bed. Her curiosity piqued, and she quickly made a cup of hot tea before settling onto her bed, her legs propped up in anticipation. Assuming the letter would contain some sort of information about her next cruise ship assignment, Clara was surprised to see it was not instructions but instead a handwritten letter.

Dear Clara,

I have been impressed with your outstanding leadership qualifications on this, your first cruise. I would like to invite you to join me for dinner in my private dining room to discuss your new assignment. I will meet you in my office, Suite 900. I am certain that you will appreciate learning about my ideas for your future. I have arranged for your duties to be covered by the wait staff during our dinner. I look forward to seeing you tomorrow evening at 8:00 p.m.

Respectfully, Captain McAllister

Clara's shock was palpable—a dinner invitation from Captain McAllister in his private dining room to discuss her future assignments.

Questions flooded Clara's mind as she grappled with the implications of the invitation. The last thing she wanted now was to be alone with Captain McAllister. Had the dinner had been a set-up to test for something like this? Could she report the captain's behavior during the formal dinner? How big were the potential repercussions of such an action, and what would happen to her if she did this?

Feeling unsure and overwhelmed, Clara wrestled with whom she could confide in.

She stared at the ceiling for a long time, sinking further into her bed as she grappled with the weight of the situation. Aware of the imminent return to duty in 20 minutes, she made a conscious effort to compartmentalize her thoughts, knowing she couldn't let this revelation affect her interactions with guests or friends.

Jittery with anxiousness, Clara stood up, slipped on her shoes, and made her way out of the room, determined to maintain a facade of normalcy. She thought of what she would tell her fellow ambassadors about her absence the previous night. What would Anna, Helen, or even Ruth say if she told them the real reason she hadn't been there? Despite the chaos in her mind, Clara made a conscious effort to retain her composure, telling herself not to let the wine dull her senses before the meeting went ahead.

Promptly at 7:59 p.m., Clara knocked on the door and was greeted by Captain McAllister's butler. He ushered her into the private dining room where Captain McAllister had been sitting. He saw Clara and rose, extending a warm welcome as he did so.

"Please join me in a glass of wine before we order dinner. Would you prefer red or white?"

Clara, feeling obligated to have at least one drink, replied that she'd have white wine.

"Thank you, Captain McAllister," Clara said as he handed her a quite full glass.

"Clara, please call me by my first name, Peter. I am sure that you are anxious to hear the purpose of this dinner. Let's start with the basics, then go into the details over dinner."

He had two papers. He kept one and handed her the other.

"On that paper is an offer of promotion within the cruise line – on my behalf. Now, before I describe the items, I want you to know that I am the lead captain of the entire fleet. Not only that, but I am also the president of the Board of Directors and own most of its stock. I do not need to ask anyone for permission to change or make decisions. If you are to accept, the promotion would be both immediate and unquestioned. Now, let's look at my proposed list."

Clara Schattinger Offer of Promotion

1. Promotion to Director of the Guest Ambassadors, which will include a 40 percent increase in salary at the beginning of the next cruise and a 10 percent increase each year thereafter per evaluation.
2. The Director and Captain McAllister will select, interview, and hire new ambassadors.

3. The Director will onboard, train, and supervise the Guest Ambassadors prior to the new hires getting assigned to their ship.
4. The Director's work will be limited to the three largest ships, serving under the direction of Captain Peter McAllister.
5. The Director will work on those assignments of the highest necessity, complexity, and diligence, as per the assignment of Captain McAllister.
6. The Director's suite will include a large private cabin with a personal bath and an adjacent office.
7. Should it be necessary, the Director will change her duties and assignments as needed based on Captain McAllister's instruction, even if the Director is serving on another ship.

After reading each item aloud, he continued, "Does this promotion look like an assignment that would interest you?"

Clara nodded and replied, "I – I'm a bit shocked by all this. I didn't know I was being considered for this promotion – I didn't even know there *was* such a promotion. But yes, I am honored by – and very much interested in – this new opportunity."

After confirming her interest, Peter emphasized the exclusivity of the offer, revealing that she was, as she had suspected, the sole candidate under consideration. He underscored the confidentiality of tonight's dinner and discussion, warning against sharing the details with anyone, including her family.

"No, I didn't mention this dinner to anyone."

"Good," the captain said stiffly. "The offer will be revoked if you share information about this promotion with anyone, including your friends and family. The contract will be given to you after dinner."

Peter rang a small silver bell, and Charles reappeared with a pair of menus. Clara reviewed the menu, then ordered a four-course meal which she wouldn't have even dreamed of getting back in Denver on her teacher's salary. Peter's order followed, even more extravagant than hers.

The meal was delicious, though Clara could only savor the delicious food so much while contemplating the magnitude of the offer before her.

After dividing the remaining wine, the captain raised his glass to make a toast.

Chapter 16

"To Clara Schattinger, the new Director of Guest Ambassadors. Congratulations."

She raised her glass and smiled as best as she could.

Dessert followed shortly after, paired with a small glass of brandy. When presented with the contract, Clara's eyes immediately ran to the overwhelmingly generous salary it offered. She knew this was indeed a once-in-a-lifetime opportunity. Peter handed Clara a fountain pen.

Chapter 17

Clara found herself reflecting on her journey over the past few weeks as she explored Seoul, Korea, with her fellow ambassadors. The city's sights and sounds provided a welcome distraction from the weight of her recent promotion and the challenges that lie ahead.

As they navigated the city's museums and art buildings, Clara couldn't help but notice the distinct architectural and cultural influences reminiscent of Chinese design. Despite the rain dampening their plans for shopping, Clara managed to find solace in purchasing a set of finger bowls, a small token of her time in Korea.

The sights of the city revealed a mix of poverty and resilience among the Korean people. Clara observed the unyielding spirit of the locals despite their humble living conditions. From the makeshift thatched houses to the laborers toiling in the rice fields, Clara gained a deeper appreciation for the resilience of the human spirit.

Venturing into the countryside, Clara and her companions witnessed a unique way of life characterized by tiled roofs and vast rice fields. The simplicity of rural living contrasted starkly with the bustling cityscape, offering Clara a glimpse into the diverse tapestry of Korean life.

During a train journey south, Clara and Steve encountered a microcosm of Korean society, from bustling marketplaces to rural communities. The train ride provided a window into the daily lives of the Korean people, their struggles, and their resilience in the face of adversity.

As Clara reflected on her experiences in Korea, she felt a sense of gratitude for the opportunity to explore a new culture and way of life. Despite the challenges that lay ahead, Clara found solace in the camaraderie of her fellow ambassadors and the shared experiences that bound them together. With a newfound sense of purpose, Clara looked forward to the adventures that awaited her on the next stage of her journey.

Clara indulged in the luxurious amenities of the hotel, particularly relishing the hot bubbling bath areas, a rare treat compared to the limited bathing facilities on the cruise ship. The opulence of the hotel, complete with attentive servants and frequent meals, underscored the luxury they provided for guests aboard the cruise ships.

Amidst the lavish surroundings, Clara received letters from loved ones, including a detailed update from Hazel about her experience as a Guest Ambassador. Despite the distance from home, these letters provided a comforting connection to her roots.

On the final day before boarding their respective ships, Clara and Steve spent their time shopping, with Clara purchasing various souvenirs and trinkets. Despite Steve's jest about her purchases, Clara remained resolute in her decisions.

As they shared a final dinner together, Clara grappled with the weight of her recent promotion and the decision to keep it a secret from Steve. Despite their bond, Clara knew that divulging the truth could jeopardize her newfound opportunity.

Walking together back to the ship, Clara and Steve shared a bittersweet moment of farewell. As Steve boarded the elevator, Clara made her way to her cabin, her mind filled with anticipation of the journey ahead and the new responsibilities awaiting her as Director of Guest Ambassadors.

Chapter 18

Clara's mind buzzed with a mixture of excitement and apprehension as she prepared for her first day in her new role as Director of Guest Ambassadors. Despite the sleepless night spent contemplating her dual identity, she felt a surge of confidence as she donned her fresh uniform and prepared to meet her team.

As she stepped outside her cabin, she noticed an envelope on the floor. When she opened it, her new name tag fell out:

Clara Schattinger

Director, Guest Ambassador

Also inside, there was a little hand-written card from Captain McAllister: "Welcome to your new position. We make a great team."

Clara felt validated in her new role but couldn't shake a lingering doubt about the captain's intentions.

On her way to breakfast, she met two new Guest Ambassadors and introduced herself as their supervisor for the first time—an exhilarating moment. With renewed confidence, she headed to the grand ballroom.

Captain McAllister greeted her with a side hug, whispering, "I'm so glad to see you this morning." She smiled warmly, taking her seat near the podium.

At 9:30 a.m., the captain delivered a commanding welcome speech, highlighting the ship's new microphone system. He saved Clara's introduction for last, announcing her as the first Director of Guest Ambassadors and praising her promotion.

As the reception concluded with coffee, tea, and pastries, Clara mingled with the newcomers, reassuring nervous Guest Ambassadors. When one asked about meals, she offered to guide them to the employee cafeteria, explaining payroll deductions and money-saving tips.

Leading the tour, she echoed words once spoken to her, realizing how far she'd come.

After the tour, Clara collected the key to her newly assigned, larger cabin. As she unlocked the door, her hands trembled with excitement. The spacious suite, a stark upgrade from her previous quarters, was bathed in natural light from a large window. With ample storage, a double bed, and—most impressively—a private office with two doors, one leading to her suite and the other to the hallway, the cabin exuded luxury. As she unpacked, she couldn't help but wonder who had once occupied such an elegant space.

Clara freshened up and restyled her hair before heading to her first meeting with the officers. Having scouted the location, the day before, she walked in confidently, filled with pride and anticipation.

Arriving early, she found most officers already seated, a buffet set nearby, and cards placed carefully arranged. Her name card was next to the captain. "Another deliberate move by Captain McAllister?" she wondered. As she selected her meal, a server offered to carry her plate, and she requested her usual—hot tea with cream.

When Captain McAllister arrived and took his seat at the head of the table, Clara couldn't help but notice the subtle gesture of his hand brushing over her shoulder. It was a small but meaningful gesture that made her skin crawl.

She noted how the server placed his meal without inquiry, thinking, "They must memorize his every preference."

The captain introduced Clara as the new Director of Guest Ambassadors, then proceeded with officer introductions by rank. He outlined the cruise agenda: departing Seoul that day for Port Tanggu, a six-day journey. They would dock for three days, allowing guests and some officers to take bus tours to Peking.

Clara took careful notes, ensuring she knew the itinerary for herself, her team, and the guests. After addressing ship maintenance concerns, the captain adjourned the meeting, scheduling the next at 7:30 a.m. the following day.

After the meeting, Captain McAllister asked Clara to stay while he spoke with other officers. As she waited, she reflected on her new role.

When he returned, he suggested they discuss her duties in her office. Following him, Clara noted his unrestricted access, realizing he held a master key to all locks.

Once inside, anxiety crept in as she prepared to take notes. But before she could react, she found herself in an unexpected embrace—his hand slipping between her camisole and blouse, leaving her stunned.

Chapter 19

On her day off, Clara explored Peking solo, eager to see as much as possible. Free from her uniform, she secured permits for Coal Hill Palace, admiring the panoramic view of the Forbidden City's yellow-tiled roofs. She marveled at the lily-filled moat, glimpsed the Winter Palace, and toured the Forbidden City's opulent treasures—gold vessels, carved thrones, and lacquered pillars.

With time running short, she took a rickshaw back to the ship, entering her suite through her private office. A mountain of mail awaited her. After a refreshing bath, she changed into her uniform, made tea, and tackled the letters—mostly job inquiries from young women. She organized them by topic, noting necessary replies.

Before her daily rounds, Clara scheduled a team meeting for the next day. Checking on her Guest Ambassadors, she found groups idly chatting and lingering in the cafeteria, their empty dishes and cigarette-filled ashtrays revealing they had been avoiding work.

Chapter 19

Taking a seat at their table, Clara initiated, "How's everything going? Any questions?"

Silence followed her query, prompting her to suggest, "Let's go around and share something you've learned about your guests today. We'll do two rounds. Begin with their cabin number and last name."

The male ambassador, appearing irritated and still smoking, hesitated, "I haven't quite caught their names and cabin numbers yet. But there's this elderly couple who've been holed up in their cabin. I hope they're okay."

Expressing frustration, Clara declared, "Raise your hand if you know the names and cabin numbers of your guests."

With no hands raised, Clara announced decisively, "Since no one seems to know, there won't be any shore excursions to Peking. You'll have a 2-hour shopping trip ashore for essentials, then it's straight back to the ship."

"Spread the word about a mandatory meeting for all Guest Ambassadors tomorrow at 1:00 p.m. in the officer's meeting room. Notices will be delivered to your cabins later tonight," she instructed before heading off to continue her rounds, informing other ambassadors along the way.

Returning to her cabin, Clara found herself amidst a sea of applicant letters, marveling at the sheer volume of hopefuls. It wasn't long ago that her own application had been another piece of paper in a similar stack. Now, she was not only chosen but also promoted.

Pondering this, she mused, "Isn't it fascinating how things unfold? Humans must learn to ask for what they desire."

As the sun set, Clara noted the guests' return from Peking. Freshening up, she applied lipstick, donned her jacket, and headed to the officers' dining room.

Familiar with most officers now, she found them kind and knowledgeable, shaped by their Navy experience. Spotting her two favorites, she approached.

"May I join you, gentlemen?"

"Of course."

She shared concerns about the crew's behavior and her plan to address it. They offered advice on motivation and proactive leadership.

Grateful for their support, Clara felt a growing sense of camaraderie, she was part of the team, no longer reliant on the captain alone.

"Thank you for your invaluable advice," she expressed. "Now, I can unwind with a glass of wine and dinner."

"You can always turn to any of the officers," they assured her. "We've formed our own little support system to navigate such challenges. You're one of us now."

With a weight off her shoulders, Clara felt empowered and prepared to confront the tasks ahead, knowing she had the backing of her fellow officers.

At 1:00 p.m., Clara entered the officers' meeting room, noting the ambassadors' silent apprehension—exactly the reaction she intended. She led the meeting with a firm lecture on training and expectations, inspecting uniforms as she spoke, reminiscent of her teaching days.

After 20 minutes, she invited questions. A brave ambassador, voice trembling, stood. "Director Clara, I apologize for my mistakes. This opportunity means everything to me, and I'll do whatever it takes to improve." Tears welled in her eyes.

After the adjournment, Clara felt both relief and tension. Back in her office, she faced her next challenge—ranking over 80 new applicants.

Approaching her office, Clara spotted an envelope—Captain McAllister was summoning her. Battling a headache, she took painkillers before heading to his office.

He questioned her about the ambassadors' meeting, leaving Clara uneasy about how he knew. When he praised her handling of the situation, citing the officers' dinner conversation, she remained wary.

Then, he attempted a hug. Clara hesitated, but he reminded her of her contractual obligation to accept such gestures. Reluctantly, she complied, realizing her role required more than managing her team—it meant navigating complex power dynamics.

The next afternoon, returning from lunch, Clara found another envelope. Assuming it was from the captain, she tossed it onto her desk before making tea. When she finally opened it, relief washed over her—it was a reassignment to another ship under Captain D'Souza, signed by McAllister.

While the move freed her from his advances, questions lingered. Had he recommended her in good faith, or was there another motive? Only time will tell.

As the ship's horn signaled departure at 4:00 p.m., Clara finalized applicant rankings, numbering each in the top corner before delivering them to Human Resources. Completing this task for the first time in her new role gave her a sense of accomplishment.

With the Director of Guest Services ill, Clara was asked to introduce the evening entertainment shows. She enjoyed a quiet dinner alone in the officers' dining room before freshening up and heading to the Grand Ballroom.

Reviewing the script in time, she took the microphone and introduced each act. Watching from the side of the stage, she relished her first chance to enjoy a performance since joining the cruise. When the final show ended at 11:00 p.m., she was more than ready to rest after a long, fulfilling day.

The ship was already docked by the time Clara rose at 6:00 a.m., greeted by the morning light filtering through her cabin window. With the Director of Guest Services still confined to the ship's infirmary, Clara knew she had a full day ahead of her. After a brief 90-minute excursion to procure some supplies, Clara returned to the ship, ready to tackle her tasks before moving on to her next assignment.

During lunch, Clara shared her observations with an officer by saying, "I saw a group of little kids with each juggling three knives and three forks." Reflecting on their resilience and ingenuity, Clara couldn't help but wish for better opportunities and education for them.

With the end of the cruise upon her, Clara had a checklist of duties to complete, including packing her belongings, finishing paperwork, tidying her cabin, and covering for the individual in the infirmary as assigned by Human Resources.

As Clara prepared for her next assignment, she couldn't help but reminisce about the day she locked the same trunk in Denver, filled with excitement and apprehension about the unknown future. Less than two years had passed since then, and Clara marveled at how much her life had changed. While she had eagerly anticipated the adventures her job would bring, she hadn't anticipated the challenges posed by individuals like Captain McAllister.

Glancing out of her cabin window at the ship awaiting her next adventure, Clara felt a surge of confidence. Securing the final latch on her trunk, she pulled it into the hallway, stealing a moment to admire her reflection in the mirror. Despite the uncertainties ahead, Clara knew she was more than capable of handling whatever her next assignment had in store.

Clara swiftly changed into a freshly cleaned uniform, neatly folding her worn one into her suitcase. Though it was a bit late for lunch, she decided to stop by the officers' dining room to bid farewell to her colleagues. However, luck was not on her side today, as she found Captain McAllister seated at the head of the table with three officers.

Upon entering, Clara noticed the surprise in Captain McAllister's expression, mirroring her own. He motioned for her to join the table, his tone chilly as he addressed her.

"What brings you to the dining room, Clara? I expected you to be packed and ready to leave your office by now. You must be out by 3:00 p.m. for the cleaning crew. However, since it's only 1:30, I suppose you may join us for one last drink," he said, his words laced with thinly veiled contempt.

Clara remained composed, declining the offer for a drink and a seat at the table. "Good-bye to all of you. It was my pleasure to have such a supportive group. Best wishes in the future," she replied diplomatically before turning to leave.

As she made her way out, Clara sensed Captain McAllister rising from his chair and approaching her from behind. She felt a shiver run down her spine as he wrapped his arm around her shoulder and whispered menacingly in her ear.

"I've given Captain D'Souza a report on your behavior. Consider yourself lucky, as I made excuses for you due to your new position. But if you dare to act the same way with him as you did with me, I won't hesitate to have you terminated. Remember, you were hired as a perk for the captain, and you were very disappointing," he hissed before releasing her and returning to his seat.

Anger and fear surged through Clara as she walked away, realizing her next assignment would demand more than professional skills—it would require navigating power and control.

Chapter 20

Clara stepped onto her new ship, greeted by Captain D'Souza's firm handshake and commanding presence. The impeccably dressed Director of Guest Services led her to a porter, who escorted her to her suite. Everything felt more formal and structured than her previous assignment.

Unlike her former officers' quarters, her new cabin was spacious, featuring a desk and a panoramic sea view. Her trunk had already arrived, so she spent the afternoon unpacking and exploring the ship, which was set for a six-night voyage from Shanghai to Hong Kong.

Reviewing the neatly organized itinerary on her desk, Clara welcomed the transparency and efficiency under Captain D'Souza's leadership— so different from the cryptic messages of the past. As she read the invitation to dine with the captain and officers at 7:00 p.m., anticipation stirred within her.

Chapter 20

To her surprise, Clara spotted Hazel and Ruth in the hallway and hurried to catch up with them, eager to exchange greetings.

"Hazel, Ruth, it's wonderful to see both of you," Clara exclaimed warmly.

However, instead of a friendly exchange, Ruth's response was icy. "We heard about your sudden promotion from Captain McAllister, along with all the perks. How did you manage that so quickly?"

Hazel chimed in with a sharp tone, "I have a guess as to why you got promoted, and it's probably just one word."

Clara attempted to explain, but Ruth cut her off. "Maybe some other time, but not today," she said curtly before they turned and walked away.

Feeling a mix of devastation, anger, and hurt, Clara realized her hopes of reconnecting with her friends had been dashed. She resigned herself to the reality of office politics and wondered about the rumors circulating behind her back.

"What did Captain McAllister say to the officers that reached the Guest Ambassadors?" she mused, determined to uncover the truth later.

Needing to refocus, Clara grabbed a quick sandwich from the employee cafeteria before rushing back to her cabin.

At the Grand Ballroom for the 1:00 p.m. meeting, she felt confident—until Captain D'Souza informed her that he couldn't stay, leaving her to lead the program alone with the itinerary. Taking a deep breath, she introduced herself and began, ignoring disapproving glances from Ruth and Hazel.

Midway through, Associate Captain Jackson, a stranger to her, stepped in effortlessly. Gratefully, she thanked him afterward, though his response was distant. Clara left the reception unsettled by D'Souza's absence and Jackson's aloofness, sensing something beneath the surface.

That afternoon, she met the Guest Ambassadors, experienced but new to this ship. Their familiarity with their roles reassured her, making for an easy, enjoyable introduction.

Around 3:45 p.m., Clara made her way to a lower deck to watch the embarkation process. It was a routine she found oddly comforting, observing the loading of supplies and passengers.

However, her attention was drawn to something unusual: ten large black barrels.

As the ship departed at 4:00 p.m., Clara stood on deck, waving to those on shore, relishing the start of another adventure.

About an hour before dinner, Clara returned to her cabin to enjoy a cup of tea and sort through her mailbox. Unlike her previous ship, where mail was left outside her door, here, she found the organization of cubbies for posted mail convenient. She made a mental note to thank the porter for pointing them out.

Reminding herself of the difference between her cabin and the officers' quarters, Clara settled in and dozed off briefly. Startled awake, she rushed to freshen up, only to realize she could have slept another hour. Frustrated by the lost rest, she used the extra time to sort through the papers from her mailbox.

As she sifted through the unfamiliar forms and information, Clara couldn't shake the thought that perhaps Captain D'Souza intended for her to take on secretarial duties, interpreting the "perks" mentioned by Captain McAllister differently. While she preferred administrative tasks over any other implications, she hadn't anticipated either aspect of the job.

Resolving to address her questions with Captain D'Souza the next morning, Clara organized the papers into stacks, preparing herself for the meeting ahead.

Clara had already located Captain D'Souza's dining room, so she knew where to go for the captain's dinner. Upon entering, she noted the same number of officers as on her previous ship. Spotting her place card far from the captain's seat, she sighed in relief and took her place.

Dinner went smoothly. It was Clara's first time seeing Captain D'Souza address a group—he was friendly, direct, and commanded the room effortlessly. Officers listened attentively, holding questions as instructed. After dinner, coffee and dessert were served, giving Clara a chance to chat with the officers beside her. They were polite and had been with the cruise corporation for eight years, but their conversation remained light, offering no real advice—just pleasant, surface-level chatter.

After dinner, Clara returned to her cabin and prepared a list of questions for her meeting with

Captain D'Souza the following morning. Her questions ranged from his expectations of her job responsibilities and how he wished her to address the pile of paper in which she had no idea of the subject matter.

Clara was up early to ensure she arrived on time for her meeting. By 8:00 a.m., she stood outside Captain D'Souza's office, but the room was dark. Unwilling to enter without him, she waited. By 8:10 a.m., she began to doubt the meeting's time or date.

At 8:12 a.m., Captain D'Souza rushed around the corner, nearly knocking her over. He glanced at her, seeming to have forgotten their meeting, then hurriedly ushered her inside. Clara set her stack of papers on the table and pulled out a chair as he sat at the head, rummaging through his portfolio. She waited in silence for several minutes before he finally looked up at her.

"Sorry for the delay, Clara. We need to make this meeting quick. I'm expecting a ship-to-shore phone call in a few minutes. What do you need to know?" Captain D'Souza said, his tone rushed.

Clara replied, "Daily, I receive piles of memos and documents in my mailbox. I do not know what you wish for me to do with the papers."

He replied with disgust, "Read them and act on the situation. If you don't know what to do, then figure it out. If you make a mistake, you can fix it later. Captain McAllister told me that you can solve any problem put in front of you. Was he mistaken?"

Clara felt a pang of frustration but remained composed. "I have no further questions," she replied curtly.

Captain D'Souza barely looked up. "Do not schedule any more meetings with me for at least three days. I'm occupied, and you're here to handle my busy work. Now, please leave."

Clara gathered the papers and left, returning to her cabin, where she spent hours sorting the documents. Some were sealed and marked confidential, which she initially chose not to open. Others detailed international trade agreements and personnel issues, some of which surprised her.

Curiosity got the best of her, and she opened one of the confidential envelopes. To her shock, it was written in Chinese. She quickly returned it to its stack but hesitated. On second thought, she retrieved the letter and tucked it into her trunk.

Clara sifted through the largest pile—guest complaints. One, in particular, made her pause. "Two male officers... too noisy during their intimacy escapades late into the night," she muttered, bewildered. "Why do I need to know this?"

She began ranking the complaints from major to minor. Minor ones included half-eaten dinner trays left in hallways, making her wonder if room stewards should conduct final hall checks. Others involved scantily clad male guests roaming after sauna visits. Some even made her laugh.

Overwhelmed, she sought guidance from Human Resources and ran into Nora, her favorite HR employee.

"Hi, Nora. I haven't seen you for a few days. You, okay?"

Nora offered a weak smile. "Just under the weather, but better now. What's up?"

Clara sighed. "Someone dumped a stack of guest complaints in my mailbox. I've never been asked to handle them."

Nora smirked. "Oh, honey, no one deals with guest complaints. The unspoken rule? We can't fix it, and we'll never see those guests again. They rarely fill out satisfaction surveys anyway, so officially, we hardly get complaints."

Clara laughed, reassured. "You're the best," she said, walking away with a grin.

Continuing her rounds, Clara addressed queries from new Guest Ambassadors, including one about using the onboard barbershop. Unsure, she returned to Nora for clarification.

After receiving confirmation from Nora that the barbershop services were available for employees, Clara relayed the information to the ambassador, who left to make an appointment.

As the afternoon flew by, Clara couldn't shake the feeling of loneliness on this cruise. Unlike previous trips, she lacked friends and felt isolated among the officers. Resigned to eating alone in her cabin, she avoided the employee cafeteria to dodge Hazel and Ruth's judgmental stares.

That evening, after enjoying a glass of wine and her dinner, Clara sorted through her mail, finding several envelopes addressed to D'Souza. Opening one, she discovered a letter detailing a shipment, further adding to her confusion about her role.

Exhausted, Clara took a warm bath before settling into bed to read letters from her parents. Among them was an envelope from the cruise ship, revealing her next assignment from Hong Kong to Manila, Philippines, a 9-day cruise.

Thrilled by the prospect of a new adventure, Clara drifted off to sleep, eager for what lay ahead.

Chapter 21

As the ship docked in bustling Hong Kong, Clara watched guests disembark—some staying to explore, others ending their journey. While some would fly home, others would take a train or transfer to another ship. Reflecting on the diverse captains she had served under, she felt grateful for the travel opportunities her job provided.

After disembarking, Clara wandered through downtown, soaking in the city's energy. Dressed casually, she discovered a charming French café tucked between towering buildings. Famished from skipping breakfast, she welcomed the waiter's recommendation and enjoyed croissants, eggs Benedict, and freshly brewed coffee.

Refreshed, she strolled along Victoria Harbor, marveling at the vibrant shops and street vendors. She picked up postcards for friends, a silk scarf as a souvenir, and fresh flowers to brighten her cabin.

Back on board, she noticed large black barrels being loaded onto the ship but paid them little

Chapter 21

attention. Instead, she was preoccupied with her new treasures and finding a vase for her flowers.

Clara was startled when she ran into Steve in the elevator.

"Oh, excuse me, I didn't see you," she said, then realized she was looking at Steve.

He smiled. "Clara, I wanted to compliment you on your presentation this morning. I have a few minor suggestions that might be useful next time." He then launched into a rambling monologue about his time in Hong Kong.

Clara nodded politely, searching for the right moment to excuse herself. As she was about to escape, Steve unexpectedly suggested they have a drink together. She hesitated.

Clara did her best to appear engaged in their conversation but spent most of the talk looking for a good moment to excuse herself and get away to her bedroom. It was much to her chagrin that Steve himself suggested they have a drink together. Clara hesitated.

"C'mon, it will be fun. You must have at least one drink each day on a cruise ship – those are the rules! Let's go to the upper deck, that one spot you talked about before that is really quiet. Over in the corner by the jukebox, right?"

Clara blushed, slightly flattered that Steve remembered this spot—she had only mentioned it in passing early on. Agreeing to meet him "around seven," she excused herself to shower and change.

Unaware of how quickly she was walking down the hallway, Clara rushed to her cabin. She took a swift, efficient shower, careful to keep her hair dry, then slipped into a freshly ironed blouse and comfortable shoes. Excitement and nerves mingled as she left twenty minutes early.

Arriving at the bar, she spotted Steve already waiting. Beside him sat two wine glasses and an open bottle of her favorite wine. Blushing again, she nearly bumped into a waiter as she made her way to the seat.

"Jeez, have you already pounded a few down without me?" he said as she made her way past the last set of people.

"I'm tired" was all Clara could get herself to say. He greeted her with a warm hug as soon as she arrived, one that lingered long enough to make her feel truly appreciated and missed.

"I needed that," Clara said, feeling her chest relax a little. She only realized how long and emotionally taxing her day had been after Steve let her go.

Clara sank into the high-top chair as Steve poured two glasses of wine and raised his in a toast.

"A true gentleman," she said, unaware of the small smile forming on her lips.

Steve held out his glass. "To our friendship," he toasted, his eyes warm and sincere.

Their glasses clinked softly in the dimly lit corner of the bar. Clara took a generous sip, feeling the wine's soothing effect more than usual.

"But that's not such a bad thing, is it?" she mused, taking another sip. The rich, fruity flavors grew more inviting with each taste.

They sat in comfortable silence for a while, savoring the wine and the peaceful atmosphere. Their quietness seemed out of place compared to the rowdiness of some of the other patrons around them, but their shared sense of exhaustion overcame any sense of embarrassment or awkwardness at the lack of initial conversation.

Finally, after finishing his own glass, Steve broke the silence. Clara noticed his voice seemed more curious and gentler than before.

"So, what's new with you? How was your cruise with Captain McAllister after you were appointed director?"

They sat in comfortable silence, savoring the wine and the calm amidst the bar's lively chatter. Their quietness felt almost out of place, but exhaustion dulled any sense of awkwardness.

Clara hesitated briefly, recalling the confidential document she signed and how it explicitly stated that the details of her director's position were never to be shared. She began with general details, but as the wine flowed and Steve listened intently, she found herself opening up.

She described the excitement of moving into her private cabin, the weight of her new responsibilities, and the challenges she faced. She spoke of Captain McAllister's strict but fair leadership, then contrasted it with Captain D'Souza's more supportive approach.

Occasionally, she worried she was saying too much, but Steve's quiet nods and reassuring smiles put her at ease. Though he never explicitly said so, something about him made Clara feel safe—like she was finally being heard and understood.

An hour had passed by the time she finished talking. The bottle of wine had been empty for a while.

Finally, feeling a bit guilty that she hadn't asked Steve many questions about his life, Clara shifted the focus. "I've been talking non-stop about myself. How about you, Steve? How have you been? What's new in your life?"

Clara and Steve's conversation started with Steve redirecting questions back to Clara, giving brief responses like "What do you think?" and "How did that go?" Clara found it unusual that Steve was sharing so little about himself, no matter how she directed the questions that way.

As their discussion moved to lighter topics, they reminisced over funny moments abroad the ship as well as their favorite experiences at each of the ports they'd gone to together. Clara laughed so hard at Steve's story about the mischievous parrot that caused chaos in the dining room that she nearly blew her wine straight out of her nose. Despite her earlier exhaustion, Clara felt glad she had hung out with Steve in the end. She had forgotten how much of a genuine connection they could have at times, and she felt optimistic about what was to come, knowing Steve might be by her side.

The next morning, the ship set sail for a seven-day cruise to the Philippines. Clara hoped for a smooth week—well-trained Guest Ambassadors, minimal issues, and little interaction with the ever preoccupied Captain D'Souza.

After greeting new passengers, she stopped by the employee cafeteria for a quick lunch, only to run into Helen and Ruth. Since they had already completed training, they hadn't attended her orientation for new Guest Ambassadors the previous day.

Clara greeted them warmly but was met with cold indifference. Trying to ease the tension, she reminisced about their past experiences together, but Ruth cut her off.

"You must have made much better memories since your promotion," she said flatly. "Why talk about the past? You're our supervisor now. It feels unprofessional, don't you think?"

Clara simply shrugged, unsure how to respond.

Chapter 21

The conversation stalled, but then Helen spoke up. With no buildup or context, she made a pointed remark about Clara's promotion, subtly implying that more than hard work had secured her new role.

That was enough. Clara quickly fabricated an excuse about work and wished them goodbye. Neither responded as she walked away.

Clara fought back tears as she retreated to her cabin, the interaction replaying over and over again in her mind. Through blurry eyes, she made her way into her cabin and locked the door behind her.

Once in her cabin, Clara was overwhelmed by emotions. Clara went straight to bed, where she sprawled out and began to weep uncontrollably. She scolded herself for being childish but still could not finally catch hold of her breath and her tears for nearly ten minutes.

The emotional release left her exhausted. Wanting to escape anywhere but where she was, she cursed herself for choosing the single occupation that made such an escape an impossibility.

It took her a while to compose herself. She had to apply extra cream to her swollen eyes and more lipstick than usual since her lips had puffed up somehow.

"Everything's going wrong, isn't it," she thought to herself as she realized she had run out of her favorite perfume as well.

However, she was able to do her evening rounds on time. For a while, she felt better. Checking for dirty trays, trash, and full wastebaskets and greeting passengers to ensure they were satisfied with the service helped take her mind off what had happened earlier.

Her rounds took about two hours, during which she fortunately avoided Helen and Ruth. In the mailroom, Clara found several envelopes in her inbox, including some from her parents and one from Captain D'Souza. She muttered something under her breath about pressure as she made her way back to her cabin.

After a quick dinner, she opened a fresh bottle of wine. She sat in the same spot as the day before, over by the jukebox, and was glad to see Steve come by and join her shortly after her first glass of wine.

Chapter 21

"Figured you would be here!" Steve said as he sat down beside her. She handed him a glass and poured another for herself.

When Steve asked about her day, Clara didn't hold back. She immediately vented about her encounter with Helen and Ruth and how they had virtually accused her of sleeping with Captain McAllister to get her current position. Steve listened attentively and asked how Clara would feel if one of them got promoted. Clara hoped she would have been supportive, given their friendship from their first voyage.

"I don't think I would have ever done what they did to me," she said, to which Steve only shrugged and mentioned Captain McAllister's reputation as a womanizer. Clara was surprised Steve hadn't mentioned this the previous night when Captain McAllister came up in their discussion. He said he had simply been trying to be a good listener since he could see there was a lot that Clara had on her mind. Clara felt unsatisfied with the response but didn't push the matter further.

Their conversation was shorter than that of the previous evening. Clara was tired and wanted to avoid too much alcohol. Eventually, Steve left, and

The Spinster I Once Knew | 251

Clara opened her mail, hoping to find some comfort in her parents' letters.

It took her a few minutes to finally open her last letter, Captain D'Souza's envelope. Inside, it was a notice of a meeting scheduled for 10:00 the following day. There was no mention of the meeting's topic. With no clear reason to worry, Clara went to sleep, hoping for a better day tomorrow.

Clara woke early, taking a hot bath to calm an unshakable nervousness. After a hearty breakfast and finishing her rounds, she dressed for the meeting and arrived at the assigned room promptly at 10:00 a.m.

It wasn't a typical conference room—it was a space she had never seen before. When she tried the door, it was locked.

Before she could knock, Captain D'Souza opened it, hastily ushering her inside. He shut and locked the door behind her, then silently motioned toward the lone table in the small, windowless room.

Two men in expensive silk suits, without name badges, sat at the table. Captain D'Souza joined them, and the three began conversing as if

Clara wasn't there. Their English was fluent, but their accents were indistinct.

D'Souza never introduced the men, nor did they acknowledge Clara. After a few minutes, he finally gestured for her to sit. Sliding three documents toward her, he instructed her to sign them. Each stated that she agreed never to disclose anything learned in this room under any circumstances.

Clara picked up the pen but hesitated. "I'm not comfortable signing this," she said cautiously.

D'Souza's expression darkened. "You've signed similar documents before," he reminded her. Reaching beneath the table, he pulled out copies of her previous agreements and tossed them onto the table carelessly.

Clara flinched, her pulse quickening.

She tried to say something else, something about how the other documents had been different, but couldn't get much of anything out. Finally, after much staring by the two men in suits, Clara reluctantly signed the new documents.

Captain D'Souza snatched the papers from Clara and replaced them with a new stack. Expecting more legal documents, she was startled to see pages filled with columns of random numbers and letters—without explanation or context.

He leaned forward. "These documents contain classified U.S. federal government information," he stated. "I trust only you with them."

Clara's pulse quickened as he continued. She was to work with this data for several hours each day, both on this cruise and the next—always in this locked room, accessible only by him.

"Work with them how?" Clara asked in confusion.

Captain D'Souza pulled one of the papers towards himself and, with a pen in hand, began silently transferring the random 6-digit numbers onto a separate lined paper divided into five columns labeled with letters A, B, C, etc.

"It's code work," Captain D'Souza explained. He demonstrated how Clara was to record the numbers under corresponding alphabetical headings, crossing each out as she transferred it.

Finally grasping the task, Clara picked up the pencil and began. Realizing the complexity, she requested separate pages for each letter and its digits (e.g., A1, A2). One of the suited men handed her a cardboard box filled with scratch paper.

As she worked, Clara developed an efficient system, ensuring accuracy. The task was tedious, demanding full concentration, but soon, she settled into a steady rhythm. The room's silence was broken only by the rustle of paper and the soft scratch of her pencil.

For over an hour, she remained absorbed in the work, finding an unexpected sense of calm. Thoughts of Helen and Ruth surfaced occasionally, but she pushed them aside, determined to focus on the task before her.

"Stop," said a low voice suddenly. Working as though in a stupor, Clara jumped a little in her seat once she heard the voice, and it was only after a few moments that she realized one of the two suited men had spoken to her. He was holding a stopwatch, which he looked at momentarily when writing something down.

"That will be all for today. You may leave now," Captain D'Souza said, taking Clara's pencil and paper from her. Despite his neutral words, Clara thought she could sense that Captain D'Souza was somehow pleased with her work by her tone. She had made significant progress, after all.

As he escorted her out of the room, Captain D'Souza reminded Clara of her confidentiality obligations. Hearing the door to the small room shut and locked behind her was both a relief and a burden to Clara. Walking back to her room, it struck Clara that she had picked up another heavy secret to carry with her for the indefinite future.

The following days settled into a routine—Clara balanced her duties as Director with long hours in the tiny, locked office. In the evenings, she often shared a bottle of wine with Steve but never mentioned her secret assignment. Noticing her slightly swollen eyes, he playfully suggested she might need glasses. She laughed, appreciating his concern but offering no further explanation.

After several nights, Steve's behavior shifted. His hugs lingered longer, now followed by tender kisses on her cheek. Concerned their relationship was becoming too involved, Clara started claiming exhaustion and heading to bed early. The excuse worked for a few days until Steve suggested they have dinner together instead.

"I'm so bored, Clara!" he teased, grinning.

She smiled. "I'll do my best to make the next dinner."

This arrangement worked in her favor. With others at the table, their interactions remained purely platonic—much to Clara's relief. It made the last few days of the cruise far more manageable.

As the ship docked in the Philippines and passengers disembarked, Clara noticed the same large black barrels from Hong Kong being unloaded. She made a mental note of the detail but kept it to herself. In the past, she might have shared it with Ruth or Helen—now, she simply watched in silence.

Back in her cabin, she changed, intending to explore Manila alone. But as she stepped off the ship, Steve waved her down from the bottom of the exit ramp.

"I know the city well," he said. "It's safer—and more fun—if we go together."

Clara hesitated, then agreed. Regardless of how things had shifted between them on the ship, she always enjoyed his company when exploring new places.

Clara and Steve spent a wonderful afternoon exploring downtown Manila, visiting the National Museum of Fine Arts and the National Museum of Natural History. Steve introduced her to famous Filipino dishes like Cebu lechon, Kare Kare, and adobo, each bursting with rich flavors.

The next morning, they started early with a visit to Rizal Park, followed by a traditional Filipino breakfast of longganisa sausage, eggs, and garlic rice. Later, they toured the breathtaking Puerto Princesa Subterranean River National Park before grabbing a quick meal of street food. By 3:00 p.m., they were back on the ship, pleasantly exhausted from their adventures.

In her cabin, Clara found an envelope from Captain D'Souza along with her other mail. She read letters from her parents and enjoyed her literary magazines. Finally, she opened the envelope from Captain D'Souza, which instructed her to meet him at 9:00 a.m. the next day for a new, similar assignment. Unlike before, Clara was not concerned. Enjoying her time with Steve, she had unwound a little over the past couple of days. She assumed the next meeting with D'Souza would involve more mundane tasks of transferring numbers and thought nothing more of it.

Chapter 21

The next morning, Clara arrived at the office at 8:50 a.m. and waited for Captain D'Souza. To her surprise, he emerged from the office with Steve, and they both looked surprised to see her. Steve walked past her without a word, and Captain D'Souza invited her in.

Inside the room, Clara noticed that the boxes and stacks of papers she had worked on previously were gone. Captain D'Souza began discussing her new assignment. He did not reference her previous assignment or what Steve had been doing in the room before her arrival.

Clara's new task required more detailed work—filing numbers rather than simply transferring them. As Captain D'Souza stood and walked to the right side of the room, she noticed a filing cabinet that hadn't been there during their previous meeting.

He retrieved three boxes of notecards, set them in front of her, and explained the process. Each card listed a person or company name at the top, followed by a string of numbers and letters. Clara was to sort them into two piles—one for individuals, one for companies—before filing them into new boxes with alphabetical dividers.

Before she could begin, Captain D'Souza placed another document in front of her: a new confidentiality contract explicitly forbidding her from discussing the assignment or the names on the cards with anyone. His tone made it clear—this was non-negotiable.

"Failure to comply will result in dismissal and serious legal consequences," Captain D'Souza stated solemnly, tapping the contract.

Clara signed without a word.

He handed her a key, explaining that she was now the only other person with access to the office and filing cabinet. She was to lock the cabinet and return the key to the desk drawer before leaving. Additionally, she was expected to complete eight to ten boxes per day—on top of her director duties.

Clara worked for a few hours before making her rounds, checking on the new Guest Ambassadors. After correcting a few mistakes, she prepared to return to filing—until she ran into Steve.

He frowned at her tired expression. "Lunch first," he insisted. "You need to catch your breath and slow down. Besides, you can only do so much on an empty stomach."

Clara hesitated, then lied. "Just rookie mistakes stressing me out," she said, forcing a smile.

During lunch, Clara remained tense despite her best efforts to appear relaxed. Steve noticed.

"You're wound up," he said.

She forced a smile. "It's the usual supervision stress," she lied, refusing to let him pry further.

After lunch, Steve lingered for another 30 minutes, ignoring her subtle attempts to send him on his way. Every minute with him meant another minute lost from her filing work, but he stubbornly stayed.

Finally, to her relief, he received a call from the bridge and left. Wasting no time, Clara rushed to the office and resumed alphabetizing the cards. She worked for hours, the stress of the tedious task only fueling her determination to get through it.

Clara and Steve's cat-and-mouse game continued for a few days after this. Steve continued trying to support Clara without knowing the details of her secret task. After denying his request for private time in her cabin one night, Steve left her alone for two days. This was both a relief and a disappointment for Clara, who managed to catch up with filing the cards in the meantime.

One night, Captain D'Souza walked into the office, surprising Clara. He was pleased to see her working at 2:00 a.m. and commended her for her effort.

As the week progressed, Clara scheduled a meeting with Captain D'Souza three days before the end of the cruise. He agreed reluctantly so that Clara was nervous when the day finally arrived.

Captain D'Souza was punctual. Clara cut straight to the chase, expressing her interest in exploring positions on other ships within the cruise line. She mentioned her six months of work experience and a promotion from Captain McAllister.

Captain D'Souza was quiet for a moment. He began by acknowledging her hard work, mentioning the 'special tasks' he had assigned her and how well she had been doing on them. He then asked her to stay with him until they reached Calcutta, India, offering her a cash bonus in addition to her salary. Aware of her friendship with Steve, he also ensured Steve would remain on the same ship until Calcutta as another incentive.

Clara agreed to stay but requested a reduction in the extra filing work, mentioning how her lack of sleep had made her more prone to potential mistakes. Captain D'Souza agreed and promised to amend her contract accordingly. She thanked him and made her way out of the room shortly after, already exhausted by the stress of the confrontation. Still, a smile crept over the right end of her mouth as she made her way back to her room.

Chapter 22

Clara, a seasoned cruise Director, found herself on the smallest ship she had ever worked on. She continued her role as Director while also taking on the task of filing for Captain D'Souza. With fewer passengers, the number of Guest Ambassadors, including Steve, was reduced. Clara's cabin, though small, had ample storage and elegant teak furniture.

As usual, Clara greeted the passengers during boarding and observed workers loading large black barrels into the ship's hold, a familiar scene she no longer questioned.

Once the ship set sail, Clara met with Captain D'Souza, who led her to a locked office—little more than a storage closet—where she would complete her filing work. Handing her keys to the office and filing cabinet, he instructed her not to lose sleep over the task.

Then, unexpectedly, he informed her that Steve would be assisting.

Before Clara could react, Steve entered, looking just as surprised. Captain D'Souza quickly demonstrated how to alphabetize the cards before giving a final directive:

"No talking. No transfer of information. Just work."

With that, he left, locking them inside to begin.

After three days at sea, the ship arrived in Singapore. With the filing up to date, Clara and Steve took a rickshaw to explore the city.

Clara was especially eager to visit the historic Raffles Hotel, renowned for its lush gardens and the iconic Singapore Sling cocktail. As they wandered, they also observed laborers carrying coal in baskets, a stark contrast to the grandeur of the colonial-era landmarks.

Their next destination was the Port of Medan, Indonesia, a three-day journey away. Once transformed by the tobacco trade in the 1800s, Medan had since become a thriving economic hub.

The ship docked for the afternoon, giving Clara time to explore the bustling street markets. She stocked up on essentials, spices, and fabric, enjoying the vibrant atmosphere.

Upon returning to the dock, she noticed shoremen loading large black barrels onto the ship—each about six feet high and four feet square, made of slatted wood with metal straps but no labels. Clara took note but said nothing, her unease growing.

After changing clothes, Clara prepared to greet the passengers once more as the ship set sail for Colombo, Sri Lanka—a six-day journey.

During the voyage, an elderly passenger fractured his shoulder, while several others recovered from food poisoning after eating street food in Singapore.

Clara and Steve spent most of their time in the locked office, silently filing documents. Despite the secrecy of their task, they shared meals daily, maintaining their companionship. Their efficiency in the office also allowed them more time to explore each port along the way.

An awkward silence fell over the pair after a few minutes in the rickshaw. Trying to fend off the silence before it became too stifling, Clara brought up the first thing that came to her mind.

"Have you noticed those black barrels we keep loading and unloading on and off the ship?"

Chapter 22

Steve shook his head.

"Really?" said Clara, somewhat shocked. "They're big enough to hold many wagon wheels or an armoire with drawers."

"I guess I've been too busy with bridge duties," Steve said, shrugging it off. "What's so special about them?"

"I – I don't know," Clara admitted.

"Well, if you find out, let me know. I love a good conspiracy."

Clara laughed good-naturedly.

"I certainly will."

Much to their disappointment, a screw came loose on the rickshaw, so the driver had to stop for a repair shortly after they left the port. Although Clara insisted they still try and get some sightseeing in before they left, Steve's logic eventually prevailed, compelling them both to walk back to the ship so as not to risk getting left behind.

Time passed quickly on the cruise. The experienced Guest Ambassadors managed well, and Captain D'Souza's check-ins were infrequent due to their competence. Clara and Steve's relationship remained friendly, with Clara setting boundaries that Steve respected.

Arriving in Colombo at 4 a.m., Clara and Steve eagerly disembarked to explore. They toured the city by car, learning about its history as the capital under British rule and visiting palm fields, spice groves, and elephants being scrubbed clean. They enjoyed a lunch of Kottu Roti, a popular dish made with flaky flatbread, spices, onions, and various toppings.

After lunch, they toured a tea plantation and factory, tasting different teas. They saw a lake with an island used by an old ruler to exile displeasing wives, a situation Clara found ironically preferable. Dinner was at an authentic restaurant specializing in Lamprais, a rice dish cooked with spices, meat, and other ingredients, wrapped in a banana leaf.

Returning to the ship, they prepared to leave Colombo at midnight. Clara ensured the Guest Ambassadors were ready for the next leg to Madras, India.

In Madras, Clara and Steve enjoyed a lunch of street food, savoring dosa and idlis. As they explored, they watched locals skillfully weaving and selling baskets and mats. Women in vibrant woven garments and simple leather sandals moved gracefully through the bustling marketplace, adding to the city's rich and colorful atmosphere.

As Clara and Steve walked back to the ship to meet the 3:00 p.m. deadline, Steve confessed that he was growing bored with his position and was exploring other job options. Having been with the company for years, the initial excitement of work and travel had faded. However, finding new opportunities was difficult due to the language barrier and the lack of classified ads in port newspapers. He mentioned he might leave as early as their next stop, Calcutta.

Clara was surprised—his plans mirrored her own. She admitted that she had spoken to Captain D'Souza about leaving, but he had asked her to stay until Calcutta to finish the filing job, insisting there was no one else he could trust. She knew this wasn't entirely true since he had assigned Steve to assist her.

D'Souza had also mentioned that the cruise corporate office was in Delhi but was uncertain if any positions were available there.

Despite needing to return to their duties, Clara and Steve agreed to continue their conversation later. Clara changed into her uniform and resumed her director's duties, greeting boarding guests and observing the loading and unloading of large black barrels. This time, she noticed the barrels varied in size, piquing her curiosity even more.

Steve assisted the bridge crew with inspections, ensuring everything was for their departure from Madras to Calcutta, a seven-day journey. They agreed to meet for a quick dinner with the other Guest Ambassadors in the employee cafeteria at 5:30 p.m., a time-saving idea from Steve that also allowed Clara to address any questions or issues.

After dinner, Clara and Steve resumed their filing work in the locked office from 7:00 p.m. to 10:00 p.m., maintaining silence as instructed. Captain D'Souza checked on their progress around 9:30 p.m., reminding them to complete the task before arriving in Calcutta. As he left, he cryptically mentioned, "Those boxes are not the entire number of boxes that needed to be completed," leaving Clara and Steve puzzled but determined to continue their work.

Chapter 22

"Keep at it," Captain D'Souza finally said, returning from his momentary trance. The two both nodded, and he left the room.

At 10:00 p.m., Clara and Steve finished their work, locked the office, and headed to the bar for a glass of wine. They then went to their favorite hidden spot to continue their conversation about future job prospects.

Loosened up a bit by a large glass of wine, Steve took a little time to bring their conversation back to their previous topic of discussion.

"If you could work any other job besides the cruise – you don't even have to be qualified for it, either. You can choose anything you want. What would you pick?"

Much to her surprise, Clara couldn't name any job she really wanted to work. Instead, she danced around the question by talking about all the jobs she was sure she did not want to work, including clerical positions or jobs in education.

Steve mentioned he could tolerate a position for a while and had saved enough money to live comfortably for a few months. They discussed their personal lives, realizing they knew little about each other despite working closely.

A few days before the cruise ended, they completed the filing task, and Captain D'Souza paid Clara her promised cash bonus. Steve's arrangement remained private. Both Clara and Steve submitted letters requesting a nine-month leave of absence, hoping to find positions at the corporate office in Delhi, India. News of their plans spread, and the other Guest Ambassadors organized a farewell party for them.

As the last day approached, Clara felt anxious about leaving the routine of the ship, the excellent salary, and the interesting guests and staff. Additionally, Clara was also concerned about her relationship with Steve. Though they were close cruise friends, she had set boundaries, and Steve respected them.

However, Clara couldn't ignore the possibility that once they left the ship, Steve might go his own way, leaving her completely alone. The thought of being stranded in a foreign country, as far from home as she could possibly be, gnawed at her. Anxiety shadowed her final days on board, making every moment feel more uncertain.

Clara did her best to push through her worries. When the final day arrived, she treated it like any other. She and Steve completed their duties, cleaned their cabins, and packed their belongings.

They had booked separate hotel suites for a few nights, giving themselves time to regroup and plan their next steps before deciding where to go next.

Around four that afternoon, Clara and Steve left the ship for the last time. As they descended the ramp, Clara gently touched Steve's arm, gesturing toward the numerous black barrels—now in various sizes—being unloaded.

Steve glanced at them for the first time but only nodded before crossing the street. His lack of surprise left Clara slightly disappointed. She lingered for a moment, watching the barrels being moved. A nagging sense of unease settled in her chest.

"If only I could see what's in them," she thought to herself, wanting to prove that there was something worthwhile in these mysterious containers. But Clara was only given a few moments before Steve called out from the other side of the street, saying he was going to the hotel with or without Clara. She took one final glance at the barrels, the port, and the ship they were leaving behind, then turned her back on it all and made her way over to catch up with Steve.

Chapter 23

As they walked toward the train station, Clara and Steve discussed their future.

"I need to get to Delhi as soon as possible," Clara said, adjusting the strap of her bag. "I need to pick up my mail from the Pacific Cruise Corporation office and see if they have any job openings. I can't afford to waste time."

Steve sighed, shoving his hands into his pockets. "You're in such a rush," he said with a small chuckle. "I get it, but honestly? I don't think I want to work on another cruise line ever again. I've had my fill."

Clara glanced at him, surprised. "Really? I thought you liked the work."

"I did, at first," Steve admitted. "The travel, the adventure—it was exciting. But after a while, it's the same thing over and over. And let's be real, the company doesn't exactly value us beyond what we can do for them." He paused before adding, "If that means waiting a while for something better to come along, so be it."

Clara nodded thoughtfully. "I get that. I'm not sure I want to stay in the cruise industry either, but I need a job lined up before I make any big decisions."

Steve smirked. "Always the planner."

She laughed. "And you're always the drifter."

As they stepped into the station, their conversation slowed. The bustling crowd and the scent of train smoke filled the air. Approaching the ticket counter, they opted for the more expensive sleeper-class tickets with access to the dining car.

"Twenty-two hours on a train," Clara mused as she pocketed her ticket. "Hope we don't drive each other crazy."

Steve grinned. "No promises."

As Clara pulled the last of her clothes from her suitcase, she turned toward the window and gestured outside. "Look at that," she said, nodding toward the Pacific Cruise Corporation office. "Right across the street. Couldn't have planned it better."

Steve glanced up briefly, then returned to his unpacking. "Lucky," he said flatly.

Clara frowned. His tone was distant—disinterested. She hesitated, debating whether to press the issue. For the past few days, his responses had been short, his presence quieter than usual.

She turned away from the window and sat on the edge of the bed. "So… what's your plan while we're here?" she asked, trying to gauge his mood.

Steve sighed as he zipped up his bag. "I don't know. Figure it out as I go, I guess. Maybe check out a few places. Walk around."

Clara studied him, her frustration growing. "That's it?" she asked, attempting to keep her voice light.

He shrugged. "What else would I do?"

She exhaled sharply, gripping the edge of the mattress. "Is this how we're really going to spend our last days together? Like strangers?" She wanted to say it and wanted to shake him out of this detached state. But she swallowed the words, forcing herself to believe it was exhaustion wearing on both.

Instead, she forced a small smile. "Well, let's at least start with breakfast. We need a plan for tomorrow, right?"

Steve nodded, but there was no real enthusiasm behind it. "Sure. Breakfast sounds good."

The stiffness in his voice made her stomach twist. Something had shifted between them, and she wasn't sure if it was the looming reality of going their separate ways—or something more.

"I'm probably going to go to the Pacific Cruise building after breakfast. You're more than welcome to come along, even if it's to look around," Clara said, hoping Steve would cave and come with her. But he only shook his head and, with a smile on his face, said he wouldn't be caught dead in the building.

"And now, it's time for me to call it a night. I hardly got an hour of sleep on that train, let me tell you," Steve said. "See you tomorrow in the lobby at nine, then?"

"Sounds good!"

He waved goodbye.

The next morning, their conversation wasn't much livelier than the night before. The only topic they managed to discuss in any real depth was their plans for the day.

Clara, eager to explore job opportunities with the cruise line, planned to spend the entire day at the Pacific Cruise Corporation office. Steve, however, remained firm in his decision not to accompany her.

"I need to explore other options," he said vaguely over his coffee.

Clara narrowed her eyes. "And where are you going to explore these unnamed options, may I ask?"

Steve only shrugged and flashed a half-smile. "Around."

His evasiveness irritated her, but she exhaled, letting it go. She wasn't his keeper, and if he wanted to wander aimlessly while his future hung in the balance, that was his decision.

Before heading their separate ways, they agreed to meet back at the hotel for dinner at 7:00 p.m.

Clara understood Steve's desire to move on had been with the company far longer than she had. Still, she couldn't help but wonder if he was taking his career prospects as seriously as he should. But they weren't romantically tied, she reminded herself. He didn't owe her an explanation.

So, once again, she kept her thoughts to herself.

Chapter 24

To clear her mind and escape the tension, Clara decided to take a day for herself. She boarded a tourist bus to Agra, eager to visit the Taj Mahal—a place her mother had always dreamed of seeing. Wanting to share the experience, she brought a notebook to record her impressions, planning to mail her reflections home.

She wrote:

"It's even more stunning than you would have imagined, Mom. The inside is breathtaking—white marble carved into delicate lace-like screens, some inlaid with semi-precious stones like lapis and jade, others with marble flowers. The floors shimmer in black, white, and yellow marble, while intricately carved pillars stretch toward the high domed ceiling.

There are marble baths and fountains, and the silence inside feels almost sacred. The tombs are surrounded by marble lattice screens, but my favorite was one carved with the words: 'Here lies the Lady Jai and Shah Jahan.' We'll have to remember that when we finally visit together.

A golden lamp burns above the tombs, illuminating their inscriptions. The guide explained that Shah Jahan and Mumtaz Mahal are buried nine feet below, their resting place adorned with floral inlays and surrounded by prayer rooms. Seven chapters of the Koran are inscribed on the walls in black marble, a testament to devotion.

After the Taj Mahal, I visited the tomb of Akbar, Shah Jahan's great-grandfather. Built from red sandstone, it has four immense gates with towering 75-foot arches. The pedestal of the tomb once held enormous diamonds—gifts from Shah Jahan's son to the Queen of England for her crown."

Clara closed her notebook, gazing at the grand structure before her. She couldn't wait to send her mother this letter, perhaps one day they would see it together.

The next few days, Clara stayed mostly in the hotel, reading her mail and writing letters to update her parents and friends. She caught up with those books she had wanted to read on the ship but could

Chapter 24

never make time for. She found it peaceful to sit in the garden for a few hours every afternoon. She did not realize how tired she was until she moved to Delhi and was finally able to get some rest.

After a few days of rest, Clara scheduled an appointment to visit the Pacific Cruise Corporate office at 1:00 in hopes of securing a position. Shortly after talking to the lobby receptionist, a short, jolly-looking man approached her.

"Please, let's go to my office."

Mr. Williams gestured toward a chair across from his desk. "Please, have a seat, Miss Clara."

Clara sat down, smoothing her skirt as she did. She studied Mr. Williams as he flipped through a folder, presumably containing her application and employment history. His round face was friendly, and there was warmth in his eyes that put her somewhat at ease.

"So," he began, looking up at her with a smile, "I see you have experience with Pacific Cruise. You worked aboard the Ocean Serenity, correct?"

Clara nodded. "Yes, I did. I was assigned clerical duties during my time there."

Mr. Williams leaned back in his chair. "That's good. We always appreciate candidates who are already familiar with our company's operations." He glanced down at the papers again. "And your previous supervisor gave you an excellent recommendation. That speaks highly of your work ethic."

Clara felt a small wave of relief wash over her. If her past performance had left a good impression, she hoped it would increase her chances of securing a position.

Mr. Williams tapped a pen against the desk, then folded his hands over the folder. "Now, tell me, Clara—what role are you hoping to secure this time?"

Clara nodded and began talking at length about her desire to expand her skillset and stay in one place longer to immerse herself in the local culture. With these preferences in mind, Mr. Williams offered her a senior office position in Bombay.

"It would open in about a month."

"Perfect!" Clara said. "That will give me time to explore Delhi, and I won't have to rush travel to Bombay, either."

The position involved managing a staff of thirty women in the typing pool and overseeing the scheduling of cruise staff for ships in the Bay of Bengal and the Arabian Sea. Clara was excited about the opportunity, which combined her cruise ship management experience with new travel experiences. She accepted the job. Mr. Williams also handed her the last paycheck forwarded mail and offered her accommodation in one of the company's guest houses in Delhi. She gratefully accepted the offer and, after receiving the information about the lease and how to acquire the key to the house, wished Mr. Williams goodbye.

As the days passed, Clara settled into her new surroundings, growing more comfortable with the rhythm of Delhi. The guest house felt like a true home—cozy yet practical, with the central garden providing a peaceful retreat in the evenings. She often found herself sitting on the front porch with a book or simply watching the world go by, enjoying the brief stillness before she moved on to her next adventure in Bombay.

Her shopping excursions were both exciting and necessary. With her new role not requiring a uniform, she embraced the opportunity to redefine her wardrobe. The markets of Delhi were a treasure trove of fine fabrics, elegant designs, and skilled tailors who crafted custom pieces to fit her perfectly. She loved the blend of Western and Indian styles she had acquired—structured skirts and blouses for office wear, light cotton dresses for casual outings, and a few embroidered shawls that added a touch of sophistication.

The biggest change, however, was her haircut. Letting go of her long blonde locks had been a spontaneous decision but one she didn't regret. The stylish bob framed her face, making her look more modern and confident. Though she struggled to style it at first, she welcomed the challenge, knowing it was part of the transformation she was undergoing.

Once again, Clara packed her belongings and traveled to Bombay to begin her new position. She left a few days early to find housing and get accustomed to yet another city and adventure.

On the first day, Clara arrived at the building half an hour earlier than instructed. She approached a woman at the lobby reception desk, who, after being told Clara's name and new position, told Clara to take a seat and wait until someone came to get her. Dressed in a simple gray dress and black low heels, with a small purse on her left shoulder and a leather briefcase with a packed lunch at her feet, Clara sat in the lobby a while, watching streams of people enter the building and wondering which of them would end up being her coworkers.

A young man eventually came up to Clara and told her to follow him. He led her to an office in the Human Resources division. Before Clara could ask him what his name was and if they'd be working together, he was out the door.

A few minutes later, Clara met Mr. Jordan, a pleasant older man who welcomed her and handed her an onboarding packet, instructing her to complete and return it to Human Resources before the end of the day. As she skimmed the document, she saw that her primary duty would be supervising a typing pool of thirty women. Her responsibilities included hiring typists, testing their speed and accuracy, tracking work hours, monitoring productivity, and overseeing attendance. Mr. Jordan advised her to be both stern and kind, explaining that management would largely evaluate her based on the typing pool's efficiency, though he reassured her that he had confidence in her abilities.

Clara asked a few questions and learned that the typists worked nine-hour shifts, five days a week, with designated breaks. The building was locked on Sundays, making it impossible for anyone to work that day. Employees were not allowed to switch shifts or cover for others on their days off. After completing a year with the company, workers received one paid week off.

As Mr. Jordan explained the strict Human Resources policies, Clara amusingly realized that she did not know how to type. The irony of managing a typing pool without that skill distracted her, and she only noticed Mr. Jordan had finished speaking when a silence fell between them. Assuring him she had no further questions, she followed him to her office.

Her workspace was small and windowless but functional, containing a desk, a side table with a typewriter, a phone, a filing cabinet, and two chairs. She was relieved that the door had a glass insert, allowing her to see the hallway. After a brief glance around, Mr. Jordan quickly moved on to a tour of the building.

On the second floor, Clara saw the typing pool, where thirty women worked diligently at their desks. The floor also had restrooms and a breakroom, where she noticed a hot plate with a coffee pot. Mr. Jordan clarified that while the workers could bring their own coffee, they had to drink it in the breakroom to prevent spills at their desks. This, he explained, was an unwritten but important part of Clara's job—one of the many responsibilities she would have to enforce in her new role.

After the tour, they returned to Mr. Jordan's spacious office, where he repeated Clara's responsibilities in a firmer voice than before. He especially emphasized the urgency of hiring three new typing pool employees to fill recently vacated spots.

"Time is money in the cruise business," he stressed. "Your previous position was easy compared to this front-end job. All you had to do was keep them happy and entertained for the duration of the cruise."

At 12:30 p.m., Mr. Jordan left for a lunch appointment, instructing Clara to introduce herself to the typing pool.

Clara spent her lunch break in the employee cafeteria, introducing herself to a group of typists, who were identifiable by their matching blue dresses. She unintentionally spoke in the loud, enthusiastic manner she had adopted from working on cruise ships. The typists responded by smiling and giggling. After about ten minutes, those women returned to their desks, followed by a group of women. Clara realized that each group had only a 30-minute break. The group was engaged in an animated discussion, and it was only as they got closer that Clara realized they were speaking Marathi, the state language.

After lunch and a brief walk outside, Clara returned to Mr. Jordan's office.

"Do you have any questions for me?" he asked.

Clara, unsure where to begin. "I became aware that the typists speak their native language to each other. I assume that they must be fluent in English to be employed here, correct?"

"As you know, our cruise ships serve numerous nationalities. Most of the typists speak three languages to work in the typing pool. They are required to be fluent in English and Hindi, but when they talk among themselves, they speak Marathi. And yes, they will talk about you in Marathi."

"I understand."

He nodded.

"Who do I contact to get a list of typing pool applicants so I can begin interviewing and administering the typing tests? And where do I get supplies for my office?"

Mr. Jordan replied, "Human Resources on the third floor can answer all your questions. In fact, you shouldn't ask me any more questions. I don't have these answers."

Clara was silent.

"Why have me ask questions if you're not going to give me any answers?" Clara thought indignantly.

"Since you have no further questions, you better leave and go upstairs to Human Resources for the rest of the day. You need to give them those papers once they're fully filled out by the end of today." He returned to shuffling papers on his desk once he finished and did not give any sign of goodbye as Clara made her way out his door.

Clara headed to the Human Resources department. "Hello, I am Clara Schattinger. I met with Mr. Jordan earlier this morning. He told me I needed to come here to get answers."

"One moment, please. I will get someone to help you," as she dialed an extension. "Mrs. Anderson, Clara Schattinger, the new hire, is here to see you."

"OK, thank you."

Immediately, a middle-aged woman opened a door to Clara's right and introduced herself with a firm handshake.

"First, call me Beth. I hope you know how difficult this job you've accepted is. But first, let me take you somewhere we can sit down and talk."

Beth led Clara to a small conference room down the hall. Once they were seated, she continued, "I don't know if you've heard yet, but we've had several people in your position recently. But I'm hoping you'll improve that trend, Clara. You have experience with cruise ships and Guest Ambassadors that I don't have, and I can teach you ways to interview, test, and train applicants to save you time and effort."

Beth leaned forward, folding her hands together, her gaze sharpening. "I've been working on revamping a lot of Human Resources lately. As

Chapter 24

you'll come to see, there are a lot of issues around here, and I aim to fix as many of them as I can. I need to know if you'll help me with this—I wouldn't bring it up on your first day unless it was that important."

Clara was taken aback but quickly realized that it would be better to be on Beth's side than against her. With impressive earnestness, she replied, "Of course I'll join you. To tell the truth, there were some big issues on our cruise ships that I wished I could have stood up against myself. Now, I can't promise too much—I hardly know how to get from my office to the lobby still—but I can guarantee that I'll give you my all if we're working toward as noble a cause as you're making this out to be."

Beth nodded. "It's a great number of worthy causes, I believe. But it will take hard work and skill—I won't deny that."

Clara smiled. "I can begin this afternoon if you're ready for me."

Beth smiled back. "Not today, but I'll make sure to call on you sooner rather than later."

Clara and Beth worked closely over the following weeks to improve procedures in the typing pool. They hired four new typists instead of three to anticipate turnover, but to their surprise, no one resigned in the following month. Productivity soared under Clara's management, which she credited to the new policies she and Beth introduced: flexible 15-minute breaks, adjustable lunch times between 11:30 a.m. and 1:00 p.m., and a monthly bonus for the top three performers. These changes fostered a more relaxed and social work environment while also reducing sick days.

Within a week, Clara learned all the women's names and tailored workloads to their strengths and weaknesses. She also engaged with their lives outside of work, and by the end of her second month, she had been invited to several birthday parties and gatherings.

After four months, Beth proudly presented their success to Mr. Jordan, showing him impressive data. However, he remained skeptical.

"We must wait another two more months before reading into anything. What will really be telling is her numbers after a full half a year," he said.

Chapter 24

Beth sighed deeply when she relayed this to Clara. "Mr. Jordan wants six months of data before acknowledging our progress," she said, clearly discouraged.

But Clara was unfazed.

Clara remained confident in the face of Mr. Jordan's skepticism.

"So be it," she said. "Let's aim for even better results then. How about we motivate the team with a catered lunch from Saffron if they improve over the next two months?"

Beth was visibly disconcerted. "Saffron?! Clara, do you know how expensive that place is?"

"I can guess. All the girls talk about wanting to go there for anniversaries and whatnot, so I figured the place wouldn't be a dump by any means."

"But we don't have the budget for that. Not even close."

"Don't worry—I'll cover it. It'll be worth every penny," Clara assured her.

Beth smiled. "I've worked here a long time, but I can confidently say that's the first time I've ever heard anyone offer Saffron as an incentive."

"I guess there's a first for everything," Clara replied before returning to her post.

She announced the incentive to the team, and the room erupted in applause.

At the end of the day, a veteran employee approached Clara as she was leaving.

"Miss Schattinger"—she stubbornly refused to call Clara by her first name despite being at least twenty years older—"I needed to tell you how much the office has changed since you got here. I've been here 12 years, and for the first time, I look forward to going to work. Last month, I earned the first bonus I'd ever received, and I think I can speak for the rest of us when I say we're as committed as ever to getting that lunch. I've never been to Saffron—can you imagine eating in the break room?"

The two laughed at the thought before parting ways.

Over the next two months, the team's enthusiasm was palpable. Clara tracked their progress on a chart, monitoring weekly production, sick days, and resignations. When she reviewed the final numbers, she was thrilled—

production had climbed steadily, sick days were minimal, and resignations remained at zero.

At the six-month mark, Clara met with Beth and Mr. Jordan, presenting the results. Mr. Jordan smirked at the chart.

"Seems you've met your goal, but don't expect me to fund that catered lunch."

"I wouldn't dream of it," Clara replied coolly.

After the meeting, Beth offered to treat Clara to dinner.

"After all, you'll be treating me to Saffron before you know it."

As they walked, Clara detailed her plans. She had reserved the largest conference room weeks in advance, secured silverware, plates, and napkins from Saffron with the agreement that nothing would be damaged, and even received approval to extend lunch to 60 minutes.

On the day of the luncheon, Beth was emotional. After delivering a heartfelt congratulation to the team, she turned to Clara and admitted, "I didn't expect you to last this long."

"But look at us now!" Clara laughed.

The two watched as the first typists began filling their plates. Mr. Jordan had declined to attend, much to their private relief.

Over the next six months, Clara grew restless. While productivity remained high, improvements became more marginal after the celebratory feast. With little left to refine, she found herself longing for the ever-changing scenery she had once enjoyed aboard the cruise ship. Though she loved her team, she missed the excitement of meeting people from different cultures.

Her desire to work on a cruise to Cairo via the Red Sea resurfaced, prompting her to request meetings with supervisors overseeing voyages to Egypt. Mr. Jordan ignored her requests, so Clara took matters into her own hands and wrote directly to Captain D'Souza. To her surprise, Captain D'Souza responded swiftly. Less than a week after Clara sent her letter, a man named Mr. Srinivasan arrived at her office.

Clara soon learned that Mr. Srinivasan was not only a friend of Captain D'Souza but also the captain of the Pacific Ganga Varanasi—the very ship she hoped to work on. They discussed Captain D'Souza and the available opportunities, but while Captain Srinivasan acknowledged Clara's credentials, he remained tight-lipped about whether she would be offered a position. When Clara pressed him for an answer, he simply said, "I'll see what I can do."

Two days later, Clara received a letter from Captain Srinivasan. He spoke warmly of their meeting and informed her that he had already returned to sea. He would be back in Bombay in a few weeks and assured her that she would receive more details about the voyage before the ship's arrival. Clara's heart raced as she read that she had been offered the same position she previously held under Captain D'Souza—Director of Guest Ambassadors. Unlike before, there was no mention of additional clerical duties. It was a clean slate.

During her weekly dinner with Beth, Clara excitedly shared the news and inquired about getting time off. Beth reassured her that Pacific Cruise Corporation employees were entitled to take a cruise once a year.

"That's great!" Clara exclaimed.

In the following weeks, Clara received official confirmation from Human Resources that she was cleared to work on the cruise ship bound for Cairo.

On the day of the cruise, she attended a staff lunch near the port, where she was reintroduced to Captain Srinivasan. This time, he was noticeably more sociable. Curious about his sudden enthusiasm, Clara soon learned the reason.

"Have you heard of Lord Carnarvon, Clara?" he asked.

She shook her head.

"Well, have you at least heard of King Tut?"

"Of course. They just excavated his tomb, right?"

"If by 'they' you mean Lord Carnarvon, then yes!" Captain Srinivasan said, his excitement contagious. He explained that Lord Carnarvon, the 5th Earl of Carnarvon, who had famously funded the excavation of Tutankhamun's tomb, would be among the ship's esteemed guests.

Clara was thrilled. The discovery of King Tutankhamun's tomb had captivated the world, and now she would have the chance to meet the man behind its funding. Throughout lunch, she rehearsed what she would say to Lord Carnarvon when they met, imagining what he must look like—completely unaware that she would never have the chance to even lay eyes on the English lord.

Chapter 25

Clara returned to her office after her cruise to Cairo. She was proud of her two teams. Each team was running without any major issues. She had dinner with Beth to get caught up on the local gossip and share her Cairo adventures.

After a few days, she was caught up with work and her personal mail. Her parents had sent several letters, and everything was normal in Denver. She wrote a long letter to tell her about the trip to Cairo and the other adventures.

The following Monday, Clara was sitting in her small office working on the evaluations for each of the typing pool women. She spent hours on this assignment because she wanted to give praise but also some advice about how to show improvement over the next year.

She heard a knock on her office door even though the door was half open. She looked up and saw two men in suits standing in the doorway.

"We are looking for Clara Schattinger. Are you Clara Schattinger?"

Chapter 25

"Yes. What is this about?"

"Come with us, madame."

"Why?"

"I said come with us. We have a few questions to ask you."

"Who are you?"

"We are investigators of the United States Federal Bureau of Investigation. We are the F.B.I."

"May I tell my supervisor that I am leaving?"

"No. You will be back soon. Please bring your identification card."

"May I bring my handbag? My identification card is in my wallet."

"Yes, bring your handbag."

Clara followed them out the front door of the building. They asked her to sit in the back seat of a black limousine. The tall gentleman drove, and the other one sat in the passenger seat. They did not say a word during the ride.

Clara was more curious than scared because she could not recall doing anything that would ever lead to an FBI investigation.

It seemed like a long ride, and since she was new to Bombay, she did not recognize which direction they were going outside of town.

Finally, they stopped in front of the United States Embassy building. She had never seen this building, but she felt somewhat safe going into the building with the gentlemen.

She carried her handbag and followed them as instructed. At the front desk, the clerk asked to see her identification card. He glanced at it and handed it to the tall gentleman instead of Clara. That made her anxious.

Again, she followed them down a long hallway that ended at the entrance of a conference room. They entered the room and there were four men dressed in suits sitting at the table. The first two men directed Clara to a chair in the middle on the side facing the four men across the table. She sat down and the two original men sat one on each side of her.

One man had the file folder which he opened and removed several sheets of paper. He slid a few pages to the man to the left of Clara. He spread three pictures in front of Clara.

Chapter 25

"Do you recognize any of the people in the photographs?"

"Yes," replied Clara.

"What are their names?"

"This first one is a picture of me and my friend, Steve Evans, at a street market. It looks like it might be in Hong Kong."

"Next."

"The second one is a photograph of Captain D'Souza. He was the captain of several cruises in which I was the Director of Guest Ambassadors."

"Alright."

"The last photograph is a picture of Steve and Captain D'Souza. I do not recognize the location from the background."

"Alright."

The men stood up and left the room. The last man told Clara to remain seated until they returned. In a few minutes, a female in a uniform entered the room and asked Clara if she would like some hot tea or to use the restroom. Clara said yes to both options. The female ushered Clara to the restroom and then waited for her. They went back to the room. The female poured Clara's tea and then sat in a chair by the door.

Clara thought, "Is she assigned to me, so I do not escape? Where would I go?"

Within 30 minutes, the men returned. They sat at the table, but this time, each man had a file folder filled with paper.

"Miss Schattinger, we are going to ask you a few more questions. Before we get started, you need to understand that this room is equivalent to a courtroom. I am Judge Martin in this F.B.I. courtroom. Please stand, Miss Clara Schattinger, to be sworn in for these proceedings. Put your right hand on the bible. Do you swear to tell the whole truth and nothing but the truth?"

"Yes."

"Please be seated. Please respond to the questions to the best of your knowledge. Also, this is a U.S. Federal investigation. You may not communicate (spoken or written) with anyone about this hearing, the questions, and your responses. Do you understand?"

"Yes."

"Have you met Captain D'Souza?"

"Yes."

"Was he your supervisor on the cruise ship?"

"Yes."

"To the best of your understanding, did he ever ask you to perform duties outside of your regular assigned duties as the Director of Guest Ambassadors?"

"Yes."

"Would you describe the assigned extra duties?"

"There were two different extra duties. One happened on the first cruise with Captain D'Souza. The second extra duty was assigned on the second cruise with Captain D'Souza."

"Please describe the first and second assigned duties."

"On the first cruise, he made me sign a document stating that I would never tell anyone about the extra duties. There were two men present when I signed the document. There were three identical documents. Is it acceptable to disclose the details in this courtroom?"

"Yes, please, proceed."

"Captain D'Souza took me into a locked office near his office on the ship. He made me sign the document so that I would never disclose the extra assignment. On the first cruise, I worked in the locked office for hours, transferring random 6-digit serial numbers of letters and numbers onto legal tablets that put the serial numbers in alphabetical then numerical order. It was tedious, and I was not able to think of anything else while I transferred the serial numbers. Captain D'Souza explained that the stack of papers contained classified U.S. Federal government information. I am calling them serial numbers because that is what they look like, but I have no idea of the source or purpose. The pads of paper that I was transferring from were typed, not hand-written. I was writing, not typing. He checked my work after the first day but not after that."

"Thank you for the description. Please describe the assigned duties on the second cruise under Captain D'Souza."

"Captain D'Souza said that I would have extra duties on the second cruise as he did on the first cruise. After boarding, he showed me another tiny office the size of a storage closet. This time, he gave me a key to the office and told me that I would be filing index cards this time. There was a filing cabinet filled with boxes of random index cards that needed to be put in alphabetical order in empty boxes. The index cards had the name of a person or corporation at the top of each card, the rest of the cards had serial numbers like what I copied onto tablets during the last cruise. This task was much easier than the previous cruise task."

"Was there anything else unusual about the second cruise?"

"No."

"Was your friend, Steve Evans, on the second cruise?"

"Yes."

"Was Steve involved in the card filing process on this cruise?"

"Yes, on the second day, Captain D'Souza said that Steve would have the same extra duty of filing index cards. He introduced Steve and told both of us that we were able to talk while working on the filing project and we could not discuss it with each other or anyone else ever."

"Do you and Steve Evans know each other from previous cruises?"

"Yes, we met on my first cruise. Steve showed the new Guest Ambassadors around and answered many questions. We got to be friends and were assigned to the same ships most of the time. We did some sightseeing together in several ports."

"Was Steve ever in your cabin?"

"Yes."

"Did he ever try to have sexual relations with you?"

"Yes, but I stopped it before we got too involved."

"Did Steve ever tell you anything about himself, such as siblings, past employment, etc?"

"No, never."

"Did the two of you talk about the future?"

"Yes, near the end of our last cruise, we decided to submit letters requesting a nine-month leave of absence from working on a cruise ship. When I told him that I was going to apply for a position with the Pacific Cruise Corporation in Delhi, Steve replied that he had saved enough money to live comfortably for a few months."

"Have you heard from him since the day that you left the ship?"

"No."

"I only have a few more questions, Miss Schattinger."

"Ok."

"My next set of questions is about another topic."

"When you worked on the cruise ships, did you ever watch the men load and unload the cargo on and off the ship?"

"Yes."

"Did you ever notice anything that looked a bit strange?"

"Yes."

"Would you describe the situation that looked strange to you?"

"Yes, I saw several large black barrels loaded or unloaded onto only the ships in which Captain D'Souza supervised. All the other cargo looked the same for every ship. It was boxes of labeled supplies, fruit and vegetables, paper, and necessary items. The black barrels were large, never labeled,

The Spinster I Once Knew | 311

and difficult for the workers to move. There were no handles or straps, and they looked almost glued closed. After the first time, I started watching every time the ship was in port. It was curious."

"Thank you."

"Did you ever see Captain D'Souza talk to the workers loading and unloading or did he inspect the black barrels within your view?"

"No."

"Did you ever see anyone try to open one of the barrels?"

"No."

"One last question for you."

"Ok."

"Did you ever hear Steve Evans called by a different name?"

"No."

"No further questions currently. The witness is dismissed now but may be called back."

The female in the uniform appeared and escorted Clara to the front door. There was a taxi waiting to take her back to her office building.

Chapter 26

Clara was deeply unsettled after her meeting with the FBI, feeling more isolated than ever with no one to confide in or seek advice from. When the taxi dropped her off at her office building, she felt nauseous but managed to compose herself until she reached her office, where she collapsed into her chair. Grateful for the water pitcher she had refilled that morning, she drank some water, reflecting on the exhausting day spent with the FBI judge and attorneys. With only about 90 minutes left until she could go home, she looked forward to eating and resting.

Beth walked by to say hello but immediately noticed Clara's unwell appearance. Clara admitted she wasn't feeling well and decided to leave early. As she exited, Beth stepped aside to let her pass. Outside, the fresh air made Clara feel slightly better, so she chose to walk home, the breeze soothing her as she pondered the day's events and wondered if the FBI would contact her again or how Steve might be involved.

After a long day, Clara picked up a simple dinner from the grocery store, cooked, and ate before retreating to her courtyard to reflect on the FBI meeting and her uncertain future. Exhausted, she went to bed early, sleeping deeply.

The next morning, a brief sense of normalcy vanished as the weight of the previous day returned. With no one to confide in, she sipped her coffee in solitude and resolved to focus on her work. If the FBI needed her, they would reach out—otherwise, she might never know what happened unless she read about it in the news.

In the following weeks, Clara reclaimed her peace. She regained her creativity, immersed herself in work, and, alongside Beth, connected with other American women in the neighborhood. Their outings to dinners, theaters, and concerts rekindled her joy. Satisfied with her work and the idea of an annual cruise, she also found solace in a nearby yoga ashram and meditation retreat. Learning Hindi phrases and practicing yoga, Clara embraced a new rhythm—one of balance, contentment, and quiet transformation.

One morning, Clara discovered an envelope on her desk, its return address bearing the ominous seal of the U.S. Federal Bureau of Investigation.

Chapter 26

Her breath caught, and her knees nearly gave out beneath her. Though she had done nothing wrong, the mere sight of it sent a shiver down her spine.

With shaking hands, she forced herself to make tea, trying to steady her nerves before facing whatever lay inside. Finally, she sat down and tore the envelope open.

The letter was blunt, cold, and absolute: she had been subpoenaed to appear at the FBI office across from the Taj Mahal Hotel, starting the third Tuesday of April 1922. The words blurred for a moment as she read on. A call would follow with further instructions. Transportation would be arranged. And most chilling of all—she was strictly forbidden from discussing the investigation with anyone. Noncompliance meant arrest.

The teacup trembled in her grasp. Clara had thought she had left the worst behind, but now, it seemed, the storm was only beginning.

Clara read the letter three times, realizing the proceedings were three weeks away with no end date given. She tried to reassure herself that she had done nothing wrong—following Captain

D'Souza's instructions didn't make her guilty, did it?

In the weeks that followed, Clara buried herself in work and distractions, filling her days with purpose to keep the gnawing anxiety at bay. A part of her longed for the proceedings to begin, just to get it over with, while another part silently wished they would never come at all.

But as time passed, she resigned herself to the inevitable. She would face it, endure it, and move forward. In her mind, it became like reading a gripping novel—one she was both engrossed in and eager to finish. No matter how intense the chapters became, the story had to reach its conclusion.

The day before the proceedings, Clara received the expected call from the FBI. A taxi would arrive at 8:00 a.m. sharp. She confirmed her readiness, her voice steady despite the nerves twisting inside her. That evening, she dined with friends, determined to distract herself, and to her relief, the plan worked. Sleep came easily, and by morning, she was surprisingly composed.

She had chosen her outfit in advance—something professional yet unassuming. After a

Chapter 26

hearty breakfast and several cups of coffee, she felt as prepared as she could be.

At exactly 7:59 a.m., the taxi arrived, punctual to the second. The ride was quiet, uneventful, and strangely ordinary. The driver, efficient and courteous, provided clear instructions: enter through the main door, take the elevator to the third floor, and wait in the witness room. He assured her he'd be waiting to take her home afterward.

Inside the building, everything proceeded as expected. She was led to a small, stark witness room—windowless, airless, and heavy with silence. A female clerk sat across from her, impassive and silent, as the minutes dragged into an hour.

Finally, Clara broke the quiet. "May I use the restroom?" she asked, her voice cutting through the stillness.

The clerk nodded, rising without a word. She escorted Clara down the hall, then waited outside the door—a quiet but unrelenting shadow.

Shortly after returning to the room, a court bailiff arrived and confirmed her identity. He then led her to the front of the courtroom, where she was instructed to sit until called. The judge asked

Clara to approach the bench to be sworn in, a process like her previous experience. Afterward, she was guided to the witness box near the judge's bench.

The judge explained that the proceedings were to uncover evidence, not a trial, and Clara would be allowed to remain in the room during the process.

As Clara looked up after being seated, she was shocked to see Captain D'Souza at one table with several attorneys, and a few feet away, Steve, sitting with one attorney, dressed in an FBI uniform—just like his attorney. The sight stunned her, and when she asked the first question, her throat was so dry that the bailiff had to bring her a cup of water.

"Do you recognize anyone in this room?" came the first question.

"Yes," Clara managed to answer.

"Please describe the people that you recognize without stating their names."

"The man at the table to my right in the FBI uniform and the man at the table to my left in the captain's uniform."

"Please state how you know the man in the FBI uniform."

"We worked together on several cruises while employed by Pacific Cruise Corporation."

"And state how you know the man in the captain's uniform."

"I worked for him on several Pacific Cruise Corporation cruises."

"Was there ever a time when you and these two men were working on the same Pacific Cruise Corporation ship?"

"Yes."

"Please describe the title that the man in the FBI uniform performed on that cruise."

"He was a Senior Guest Ambassador."

"And the other man?"

"He was the captain of the ship."

"Was everyone employed by Pacific Cruise Corporation on the ship required to report to the captain?"

"Yes."

The questioning continued for over an hour, with only a ten-minute break. Clara remained composed, though the questions were relentless. Afterward, there was a 60-minute lunch break, during which Clara stayed quiet and focused, knowing she would be back in the witness box soon.

After lunch, the questioning resumed for another hour, with a brief ten-minute break. Clara sat in the witness box the entire time, answering each question carefully. Finally, around 4:00 p.m., the judge concluded the day's proceedings and announced that they would resume the following day at 9:00 a.m.

Clara stood up from the witness box, weary, and was escorted by the same female clerk to the waiting taxi outside the building. As soon as she settled into the back seat, she collapsed, exhausted, despite having sat all day in court. The mental strain weighed heavily on her.

Once home, Clara wasted no time. She changed into comfortable clothes and took a short walk, hoping the fresh air would help clear her head. After returning, she poured herself a glass of wine and went out to the patio with her notepad, feeling the need to process the day's events. Even though she knew she couldn't bring any notes or questions into the courtroom, writing down her thoughts felt like a way to ease her mind and prepare for the following day.

She began jotting down her thoughts, trying to make sense of everything. She wondered if she had been set up from the very beginning of her employment with Pacific Cruise Corporation. Did they see her as an easy target because she was a teacher? And why was Steve, of all people, involved with the FBI? What role had he been playing in all of this?

Her mind raced with questions: Why had she been promoted? Was there a bigger plan in place for her? What was Captain D'Souza's role in the entire situation? When would Steve and the captain be questioned?

As the list of questions grew longer, Clara realized the futility of trying to find answers on her own. Frustrated, she decided to put the notepad away and head to bed, knowing she would need all her strength for the next day.

The next morning, the taxi arrived promptly, and Clara was ready for another day of questioning. As before, she entered the building and was escorted to the courtroom on the third floor. This time, she noticed an additional table had been set up next to the two from the previous day. The bailiff approached her and said, "You may sit at this table today instead of the witness box near the judge."

"Will I be questioned today?" Clara asked.

"I cannot answer that question. The judge will determine the questions."

"Thank you," she replied, taking her seat.

Soon, everyone entered the room, and the bailiff announced, "All rise for the entry of the judge."

"Please be seated," the judge instructed. Once the room settled, the judge announced, "Today's proceedings will focus on Captain D'Souza."

Since Clara had already detailed the extra tasks Captain D'Souza had her perform in secret during their first cruise, the judge started the questioning from that point. The bailiff called Captain D'Souza to be sworn in. After the oath, the judge began the interrogation.

"Captain D'Souza, would you please explain why you asked Miss Schattinger to fill numerous

Chapter 26

pages on tablet paper to organize random codes from other pages of papers?"

Captain D'Souza looked uneasy but responded, "I am embarrassed to admit that I'm not a very organized person. Instead of keeping a proper system for maintaining the supply inventory of the ship, I would jot down number codes from each box of supplies. Over time—months and several cruises—I had piles of disorganized codes that made no sense. I realized I had to submit an inventory request to the Pacific Cruise Corporation every six months, and I had no way to determine what I needed to order. Clara seemed very organized, so I thought she could help me clean up my mess."

The judge pressed on, "Did you make her sign documents stating that she could never disclose this extra task to anyone, or she would be dismissed immediately?"

"Yes," D'Souza admitted. "If she told anyone, I knew I'd be dismissed from my position. By threatening her, I thought I could save my job."

"And why were there two unknown men in the room when she signed these documents?" the judge asked.

"Oh, those men were friends of mine. They were there to make Clara feel threatened. They didn't have any role in fixing my disorganized situation."

"Was Miss Schattinger able to complete the supply inventory task before the end of the cruise?"

"Yes," D'Souza said. "She finished it before the cruise ended. I used her organized tablet sheets to submit the inventory request two days ahead of the deadline. She saved both my position and her own."

The judge paused before saying, "Thank you. I have no further questions for you, Captain D'Souza, currently."

Clara sat in silence, processing the exchange, as Captain D'Souza returned to his seat.

Clara made a mental note of Captain D'Souza's appearance—damp with sweat after his questioning. His obvious distress intrigued her, and she wondered if anyone else in the courtroom noticed it as well.

After a brief ten-minute break, the judge resumed the proceedings and announced that he had a few questions for Mr. Steve Evans. The

Chapter 26

Bailiff swore him in, and the judge began the questioning.

"Mr. Evans, how long have you been employed by the FBI?"

"Twelve years," Steve replied, his voice steady.

"And how long have you been impersonating a Guest Ambassador for the Pacific Cruise Corporation?"

"Four years," Steve answered without hesitation.

"What is the reason for your FBI assignment on Pacific Cruise Corporation ships?"

Steve explained, "I was chosen for this role because of my background. I have a degree in mechanical engineering and learned sailing from my father. My dual role allowed me to work on the bridge as well as monitor the activities of both employees and passengers. There's often illegal activity at sea, particularly given the brief stops in foreign ports."

The judge leaned forward slightly. "Did the FBI specifically suspect this behavior on Pacific Cruise Corporation ships?"

"No," Steve clarified, "the FBI oversees activities across multiple cruise lines, not just Pacific Cruise Corporation."

"Were you looking for anything in particular with Captain D'Souza's ships?"

"No, we keep an eye on all ships equally," Steve replied, maintaining his composure.

The judge shifted focus. "How did you come to know Miss Clara Schattinger?"

"We met on her first cruise. We were both working as Guest Ambassadors under Captain McAllister," Steve said. "It was the first time Pacific Cruise Corporation employed female Guest Ambassadors, and part of my assignment was to observe how they were accepted by the crew and passengers. Clara was a bit older than the other female ambassadors, and we naturally became friends, acting as informal leaders for the younger recruits."

"Did you notice anything unusual about Miss Schattinger's first cruise?"

"Yes," Steve said, leaning slightly forward. "As I mentioned, it was the first cruise with female Guest Ambassadors under Captain McAllister, who had a reputation as a 'ladies' man' among passengers. The Pacific Cruise Corporation specifically wanted me to monitor his behavior, particularly around the female crew members, along with my other duties."

The judge's gaze sharpened. "And did you observe anything of concern?"

Steve nodded. "Yes, Captain McAllister immediately took an interest in Miss Schattinger. At the first formal welcome dinner, he instructed the server to place his name card next to hers, and for the rest of the evening, he only engaged in conversation with her."

"And how did Miss Schattinger respond to this attention?" the judge asked.

"Clara handled it with grace," Steve said, with a hint of admiration in his voice. "She was mature and experienced enough to avoid his advances without causing a scene, but Captain McAllister didn't give up throughout the cruise. He kept finding ways to be near her. It became clear that his attention was unwanted, but she navigated the situation skillfully."

The judge leaned back in his chair. "Did you take any action regarding Captain McAllister's behavior?"

"Yes," Steve replied. "At the end of the cruise, I recommended to the Pacific Cruise Corporation—and the FBI—that Clara be reassigned to a different ship to avoid further issues."

"And did the reassignment happen?"

"Yes," Steve confirmed. "When the FBI suggests a change, it's in the best interest of the cruise line to comply. Clara was promoted to Director of Guest Ambassadors and reassigned to Captain D'Souza's ship."

The judge paused, then announced, "We will now take a lunch break. Food is available in the adjacent room, the same as yesterday. Remember, conversation with anyone is strictly forbidden during these legal proceedings. We will reconvene at 1:00 p.m."

As the courtroom emptied, Clara absorbed the new information. Steve had been monitoring her since her first cruise, and his role within the FBI had been far more intricate than she ever suspected. The pieces were beginning to fall into place, yet many questions remained.

Clara wasn't hungry, so she chose an apple and a cup of coffee during the lunch break. She

Chapter 26

found a quiet spot outside on the balcony, away from everyone, and sat alone, thinking over the morning's revelations. Steve's involvement with the FBI and his apparent concern for her safety during the cruise was starting to add another layer to the tangled web of her experience.

When the afternoon session began, the judge called Captain D'Souza back to the stand for further questioning. As the bailiff moved to swear him in again, the judge waved it off. "One per person is sufficient for the entire legal proceedings," the judge remarked.

The judge wasted no time getting to the heart of the matter. "Captain D'Souza, can you explain the extra tasks Miss Schattinger performed during the second cruise? I believe she mentioned filing index cards."

"Yes, Judge," Captain D'Souza responded, his voice more measured this time. "The task was like what she did before, helping me get organized. This time, instead of supplies, it was the gift shop inventory—trinkets, souvenirs, clothing, and jewelry. Each card represented items in the shop's stock."

The judge furrowed his brow. "Why wasn't the gift shop responsible for its own inventory?"

Captain D'Souza shifted uncomfortably. "That's a question for the Pacific Cruise Corporation. I don't know why they don't handle it themselves."

"And why were some of these filing cards written in different languages?" the judge continued.

Captain D'Souza sighed. "Because we stock souvenirs from the various countries we visit at different ports. The cards reflect the origins of the goods."

The judge looked stern. "Now that you're caught up on your inventory, what measures are you taking to stay organized?"

Captain D'Souza, visibly embarrassed, answered, "Judge, this situation will never happen again. I've learned my lesson."

After a brief ten-minute break, the judge turned his attention back to Steve. "Mr. Evans, was Captain D'Souza aware of your FBI role on his ship?"

Chapter 26

"Yes, Judge," Steve confirmed. "The FBI informed him of my assignment."

"And why did you involve yourself in the filing process Miss Schattinger was doing for Captain D'Souza?" the judge asked, eyeing Steve intently.

"I was concerned for her safety," Steve replied. "I wanted to understand exactly what Captain D'Souza was having her do behind a locked door. It didn't seem appropriate, and I needed to make sure she wasn't in any danger."

"Did Captain D'Souza question your request?" the judge asked.

"No," Steve said. "I reminded him that I represented the FBI, and that was enough."

The judge nodded thoughtfully. "I see. No further questions for today. We will resume tomorrow at 9:00 a.m. The court is adjourned."

As the proceedings ended for the day, Clara's mind was racing. She had been thinking all afternoon about something that didn't sit right with her. Instead of leaving the courtroom, she made her way to the judge's office door and knocked.

Without looking up, the judge called out, "Come in."

Chapter 27

Clara took a deep breath and walked into the judge's office. The room was quiet. Tall windows that let in the late afternoon light. The scent of polished wood and old books permeated the office.

Judge Wexler, a man in his early sixties with sharp features and graying hair, looked up from a stack of papers on his desk. He appeared surprised to see Clara standing in his doorway.

"Please, have a seat, Miss Schattinger. How can I help you?" His voice was calm but carried the weight of someone used to commanding attention.

Clara nodded, moving carefully toward the dark leather chair in front of his desk.

"Judge, I am concerned about an issue," she began as she seated herself. Her voice was steady, but her hands trembled slightly in her lap. "Do you have a few minutes?"

"Yes, of course," Judge Wexler said, leaning forward, his eyes narrowing with interest. "What seems to be the problem?"

"I believe that Captain D'Souza lied to you."

The judge's expression shifted slightly, his surprise giving way to curiosity.

"Tell me more."

Clara took another deep breath, gathering her thoughts.

"The first time I was assigned to Captain D'Souza's ship; I was at the boarding level. That's where we guest ambassadors usually go to greet the passengers as they board. While I waited for them to arrive, I noticed something unusual being loaded onto the ship by the Shoremen and a few crew members. They were loading large black barrels, and the sight immediately struck me as odd."

Judge Wexler raised an eyebrow. "Odd? In what way?"

"Well," Clara hesitated for a moment, "I was still new to working on cruise ships then, but during my time on Captain McAllister's ships, I never saw barrels like that being loaded onto any vessel. They were big, heavy-looking things, and all of them were entirely black."

"Do you remember seeing any shipping tags on them?" the judge asked.

"No," Clara admitted, "I didn't see any shipping tags, but I couldn't see all sides of the barrels, either, because of where I was standing."

"And is this the only time you saw these black barrels?"

"No, sir," Clara replied, her brow furrowed. "That's the strange part. I saw them again at the next port, too, and after that, I made it a point to keep an eye out every time we docked somewhere. Each time we did, I saw those same barrels. Sometimes, they were being loaded onto the ship. Other times, they were being unloaded. It happened at every single port."

The judge frowned. "Did you ever manage to get a closer look at the barrels? Maybe you saw something on them at one of the ports that could help us identify them?"

Clara nodded.

"After noticing them a few times, I started trying to get closer looks at them whenever I could. To do this, I would walk to the far end of the deck, where I could get a better view of the part of the ship where the barrels were loaded and unloaded.

The first time I tried to get a better look like this, I saw that there were black straps around the barrels, running from top to bottom. They looked like they were made of leather, and I'm pretty sure there was something engraved on them—maybe numbers or letters—but I couldn't make out exactly what they said. It was too far."

Judge Wexler tapped his pen against the desk, his mind clearly working through the details. "Did you ever mention this to anyone on the crew?"

"Yes, I pointed it out to Steve once. As you know, we sometimes went sightseeing together at the different ports. I mentioned it to him one time as we were leaving the ship, but he didn't seem concerned. At the time, I didn't think much of it. But now…"

"But now what, Miss Schattinger?"

"Well, I didn't know that Steve was working for the FBI then. Honestly, I thought then that Steve didn't take any interest in the barrels because he didn't want to get mixed up in whatever was going on. A lot of guest ambassadors are like that. They know some illegal stuff goes on during those cruises sometimes, at the ports or on the boat, and that it would cause a fiasco if they reported it to the higher-ups. Hell, doing that could even get them fired if they can't clear themselves as accomplices well enough. So, when Steve didn't take an interest in the barrels, I dismissed it as the sort of attitude any guest ambassador would take in the situation. But now, knowing that he wasn't a regular guest ambassador by any means, I can't help but wonder if Steve already knew something about those barrels."

Judge Wexler's expression softened slightly.

"Miss Schattinger, I appreciate you taking the time to bring this to my attention. What you've observed may indeed play a crucial role in uncovering the truth."

"Do you think Steve knew?"

"Unfortunately, it is not my place to tell you what I think about such matters," the judge replied. But he must have seen the defeated look creeping over Clara's face, for he added, "Still, thank you for having the courage to speak up. It was very noble of you to go out of your way like this to help move the case forward when you have so little stake in it. I cannot express my appreciation enough. Now then," Judge Wexler said, rising from his chair, "You'll have to excuse me for asking to be alone. I have a lot to review still."

He walked towards the door and opened it for Clara. She got up and followed.

"I'll see you in the morning, Miss Schattinger. Try to get some rest, and thank you again."

"Thank you," Clara said as she made her way out of the office, "I'll try."

As she left the judge's office, the corridors of the courthouse seemed quieter than ever, the echoes of her footsteps bouncing off the walls. The day had been long, and tomorrow promised to be even longer.

-

The next morning, Clara was picked up by the same taxi driver, who again greeted her with the same knowing nod. The city was buzzing with morning traffic so bad that the maneuvers of the driver jilted Clara back and forth in their seat multiple times.

"Sorry," the driver apologized after a particularly rocky lane change, "but I have to be driving like a madman now if I'm going to get us there on time in this traffic."

Chapter 27

When Clara did not respond, the driver thought she was giving him the cold shoulder in her disapproval and murmured something inaudibly. However, the truth was that Clara had not heard what the driver said nor noticed the car's movements as anything out of the ordinary. Her mind was elsewhere completely throughout the drive, and she was quite confused when the driver hastily dropped her off in an illegal parking spot a bit closer to the door than usual.

But the looming weight of the upcoming proceedings abated for only a moment as she made her way towards the FBI building.

She was escorted by a quiet, stern-faced agent up to the third floor and was, in fact, almost out of breath when she was finally seated in the same chair as before. The room was still and dimly lit, with the hum of the air conditioning being the only sound. Clara checked the clock on the wall—it was one minute before 9:00 a.m.

"We were barely on time even after basically running all the way here," Clara thought to herself, staring at the polished wood of the table, waiting for the others to arrive. But her thoughts again raced too much for her to put together anything of what had happened, and it took just a handful of seconds for the court doors to swing open and the bailiff to enter the room.

"All rise." Clara stood, her nerves steadying themselves. Judge Wexler entered through the same door she had used the previous afternoon. His robes flowed behind him as he moved with purpose to his seat. His eyes briefly met Clara's before he addressed the room.

"Be seated," he said briskly as he himself sat down. "The questioning will begin with Mr. Steven Evans this morning."

Steve, who had been seated near the front, stood and nodded.

"Yes, your honor," he said, his voice calm and measured. Even in those three words, Clara could discern a sort of collected quality to Steve's voice, which reminded her much more of the judge's tone of voice than D'Souza's. He exuded a quiet strength, and she assumed he had been briefed about the questions he would face today. He didn't look nervous at all, and Clara couldn't help but notice how handsome he looked in his FBI uniform—his dark hair neatly combed, his posture straight and confident.

Chapter 27

"Mr. Evans, when you were assigned by the FBI to investigate Captain D'Souza's ship, were you given specific instructions on what to investigate?"

"Yes, your honor," Steve said.

"Please elaborate on the nature of these instructions."

"The FBI's assignment was simple: determine if Captain D'Souza was involved in any smuggling operations. I was not given any specifics beyond that. My job was simply to investigate any suspicious activity aboard the ship that might have pointed that way."

"And what did you find during your time on the ship?" the judge asked, leaning toward Steve slightly as he did so.

"I had been assigned to Captain D'Souza's ship several times over the past few years. During those assignments, I found nothing out of the ordinary, nothing to suggest illegal activity. But the FBI was persistent—they were convinced there was something going on, so they assigned me one last time."

"And on this last assignment, did you find anything suspicious?" the judge pressed.

Steve nodded. "Yes, your honor, but I must give credit where it's due. Miss Clara Schattinger was instrumental in this investigation. She approached me several times, telling me about large black barrels she noticed being loaded onto or off the ship at the various ports. At first, I didn't think much of it—after all, I had never seen anything like the barrels she described. But then, one day, as we were disembarking for a brief sightseeing tour, Clara pointed them out to me."

He glanced briefly at Clara, offering her a small, appreciative smile.

"Please describe the barrels," the judge said.

"The barrels were large and black, with several leather straps wrapped horizontally around them. The straps appeared to have something engraved on them, but we were too far away to make them out clearly. I must admit I hadn't paid much attention to them until Clara pointed them out that day. I want to apologize to her for that."

Clara felt a small flush of warmth at his words but did her best to keep a stoic face up, knowing the whole court was now looking at her.

"Did you notice anything else unusual about the barrels?"

Chapter 27

"Yes, your honor. The men loading and unloading the barrels were not part of the regular ship's crew. They wore different uniforms, which immediately raised my suspicion. After our sightseeing tour, I returned to the ship and made my way over to the cargo area. There, I found about twelve of those black barrels stored in the hull. I casually asked a few crew members about them, but their responses were vague—they all claimed they had no idea what the barrels contained. But their body language told me otherwise, I thought. I knew these men well enough to tell when they were lying."

"What did you do next?"

"I inspected the barrels more closely and copied down the engraved serial numbers and letters on six of the barrels," Steve replied. "Then I went upstairs to the tiny, locked office where Clara was working on the extra tasks Captain D'Souza had assigned her. There, I located the index cards that matched the serial numbers and letters I had copied."

"And what did the cards say?"

Steve's brow furrowed slightly.

"The cards were written in Hindi. Luckily, I've lived in India long enough to understand some basic Hindi. From what I could tell, the writing on the cards seemed to mention jewelry and precious metals a lot. I didn't take the cards out of the office, but I thought this much was clear after checking a dozen or so cards."

"What did you do after discovering this?"

"I immediately went to the bridge and sent a coded telegram to the FBI at an undisclosed location. They verified receipt of the message by sending back a coded telegram. Fortunately, at the next port, the ship was scheduled to be docked for two nights. During that time, the FBI was able to get undercover agents working at the dock. As the fabricated ship crew members unloaded the barrels, the FBI agents were able to load the barrels onto a truck. The fabricated crew members were accustomed to that protocol, so no one was suspicious. By the time that barrels were loaded onto the truck, the FBI agents secured the barrels as evidence and drove away."

"Then what happened," the judge inquired.

"My FBI assignment was complete. I returned to the ship to serve as a Guest Ambassador for the remainder of the cruise.

The judge thanked Steve for his FBI service and gave a nod of thanks to Clara.

The judge said, "Bailiff, please approach the bench."

As the judge spoke in a soft tone, the bailiff nodded several times.

The judge stayed seated as the bailiff left the courtroom. Within less than a minute, the bailiff returned with three uniformed FBI officers entered the room and approached Captain D'Souza, who sat in silence. Without a word, they handcuffed him and escorted him out of the room. Captain D'Souza offered no resistance, his face unreadable as he was led away.

"These legal proceedings are now concluded," the judge said. "Captain D'Souza's trial will begin in a few days. Mr. Evans, Miss Schattinger, you are both dismissed. Your testimonies have been recorded. As I mentioned before, do not discuss these proceedings with anyone—family, friends, or the press. There may be reporters waiting outside. Ignore them and proceed directly to your assigned taxis."

Clara exhaled deeply, the tension finally releasing from her body. She exchanged a quick smile with Steve as they left the courtroom. Outside, they parted ways—Clara to her taxi and Steve to his.

Life returned to normal for Clara over the next few weeks. She kept her promise, never discussing the case with anyone. She continued her work for the Pacific Cruise Corporation, but after six months, she found herself restless. The excitement of the past months had made her realize there was so much more to explore. With a sense of finality, she submitted her resignation and purchased a train ticket to Jerusalem, ready for her next adventure.

Chapter 28

In Jerusalem, Clara's journey began in Bethlehem, where she visited the Church of the Nativity. The place deeply resonated with Clara. As she stood inside the ancient basilica, gazing at the supposed birthplace of Christ, a renewed sense of wonder overcame her. It had been nearly a year now since she'd gone sightseeing with Steve, and she had since become somewhat numbed to the novelties of her travels after settling down in India. But now, immersed again in a place oozing with novelty and historical significance, she felt her spirit for adventure rekindled.

From there, Clara ventured to the Mount of Olives. Here, the panoramic views overlooking Jerusalem stirred a sense of serenity in Clara. This was mixed with an almost dream-like emotion, which pervaded throughout most of her time in Jerusalem. The city was filled to the brim with settings and monuments she had only read about in religious texts. Though Clara had always told herself she'd travel to Israel someday, being there in person felt almost unreal to her, a feeling which further enhanced her wonder with each passing sight.

The Garden of Gethsemane was next, followed by retracing the steps along the Via Dolorosa, the Stations of the Cross, with markers commemorating significant moments of Christ's final journey. She was particularly moved by the prison where Christ was believed to have been held before his crucifixion. Clara then finished her day by visiting the Chapel of Mary Magdalene, a beautiful structure nestled in the path of their tour, before returning to the hotel to sleep.

The next day, she headed towards Damascus and the Jewish Wailing Wall. Getting there required a boat trip along the Dead Sea, at the end of which Clara gave into her curious temptations and took a deep sip of the sea's water. A local laughed gaily as he watched Clara immediately spit the water out and cough a little, the saltiness overwhelming her taste buds and burning her throat.

After seeing the wall, Clara went to see Solomon's Temple. She then spent her time wandering through several other nearby temples, each more impressive than the last. Finally, sunburnt and exhausted, with aching feet and a thin layer of dried sweat layered over most of her body, Clara returned to her hotel for another well-deserved rest.

The next morning, Clara left for Haifa, where she boarded a bus to Beirut before catching a ship to Athens. Along the way, they made a brief stop at the small island of Rhodes, where the clean, narrow streets paved with cobblestones impressed her. By now, she had come to realize how much she enjoyed the independence of traveling alone. At times she missed not having Steve alongside her as before, telling her about this and that, guiding her to spots she might never have even thought to visit if not for his advice. But, often, she now found herself wondering how she had not always traveled like this before. She reveled in the freedom of doing whatever she wanted whenever she pleased—never needing to rush or wait for anyone else.

Upon arriving in the port of Piraeus, Clara hired a driver to take her to the Acropolis, where she stood in awe of the magnificent ruins and the towering Doric columns that had withstood the test of time. Her travels then took her by bus to Smyrna and from there to Constantinople, where she was impressed by the city's beautiful harbor and rich history. She visited many museums in Constantinople as well, throughout which she saw a wealth of artifacts that only could compare to those she had encountered in Japan. She then concluded her time in the city by visiting the Hagia Sophia and its beautiful dome and intricate mosaic work, enriched by the building's centuries worth of religious history.

Understandably exhausted from her travels, Clara decided to take a short break before continuing onwards. From Constantinople, she booked a voyage to Brindisi, a port city on the Adriatic Sea in southern Italy, where she planned to find an inn to stay at for a few days to recharge. However, after a tumultuous journey across the Mediterranean, during which Clara developed a painful infection on her face, Clara was forced to spend an entire two weeks at a beachside inn after arrival. This delay would've likely been even longer, too, had the innkeeper not helped Clara in her recovery. An older, portly woman, the innkeeper helped Clara find medicine and ointments for her face, which throbbed with pain for well over a week. At times, the pain was so bad that she could not get out of bed, so the innkeeper had to bring Clara her supper in bed multiple times.

She nearly telegrammed home for help after her worst night of pain but ultimately held out until the infection finally began to clear. However, once the pain was finally gone, Clara found her eagerness to explore any portion of the town wholly absent. The place had become stained with her suffering, and Clara only regretted saying goodbye to the innkeeper after buying an overnight train ticket to Naples.

> 1922 Monday 30, Oct.
> I had a miserable trip on the "Leopolis" Got the deck washed on to me every A.M. and got my face infected — When I landed

After another day of rest and a few restorative meals, Clara attacked Naples with a vengeance. That morning, Clara felt an intense desire to make up for lost time, and though her face began to ache again from the salty sea breeze, Clara spent the next day visiting the city's museums, roving through aisle after aisle of Renaissance and Baroque art. She then spent the afternoon wandering through bustling wine shops and bakeries and strolling along the street cafes and theaters that dotted the city as the sun began to set. It was with a sense of pride that Clara returned to her hotel that night, mentally listing each place she had seen and each enjoyment she had had.

The next day, Clara realized that, in her eagerness to see the city, she had somehow exhausted nearly everything she'd wanted to do or see in Naples in a single day. She toured some of the city's churches that morning—both large and small. Then, seeing it was the last item on her checklist still untended, she visited the ruins of Pompeii. However, Clara found that she was glad to have nothing else left to her by then. This kept any sense of urgency at bay as she spent most of that second day touring the ashen city, where remnants of homes, theaters, and even human forms frozen in time gave her an appreciation of how fickle a thing time can be.

"I could've gotten here one week ago to see these ruins or been handicapped ten years in that small town before finally making my way here," Clara thought to herself, her eyes stuck to a pair of

Pompeiians lying beside one another. "They'd have been here then, and they'll be here long after I'm gone." And so, it was with a good deal of unburdening that Clara boarded a train bound for Rome that night.

Rome exceeded Clara's expectations like no other destination she had visited yet. From the very first foot, she stepped off her train, Clara found herself utterly captivated by the city's history, art, and architecture. During her time in the great city, she visited the Catacombs, the Colosseum, the Baths of Caracalla, and the Vatican, the last of which left the greatest impression of them all on her.

After a week in Rome, Clara boarded another train, this time headed for Florence. There, she spent hours in the Uffizi and Pitti galleries, soaking in the works of the great masters—Raphael, Rembrandt, Botticelli, and countless others. Next came Venice. There, she visited St. Mark's Basilica, and the Bridge of Sighs left her with an impression unlike any other in her travels, despite all the places across the world Clara had been to in those last few years. Imagining the condemned prisoners making their final journey across the enclosed passage, never seeing freedom again, left

Clara both deeply shaken and deeply fascinated. She found herself hanging on every word of the tour guide's spiel as they described the grim details of the execution site, where three holes in the floor drained away the blood of the beheaded prisoners.

Leaving Venice behind, Clara took a train to Milan, where she saw da Vinci's iconic painting, "The Last Supper." From Milan, Clara continued her journey by train into Switzerland, which she recognized with an excited gasp as the Alps came into view from her cabin's window. There, she visited the picturesque villages bordering the tranquil waters of Lake Como and Lake Lugano. Many times, the sights of the Alps and the expansive valleys they gave way to reminded her of postcards from back home. One evening, watching the sunset on one of these valleys, Clara took a moment to pride herself in thinking how few other Fairplay residents had traveled this far. For them, these valleys would forever remain the distant lands of postcards. For Clara, they had been a reality.

Continuing her travels, Clara crossed into Alsace-Lorraine, the region bordering France and Germany. After a brief stop there, she boarded a train bound for her next grand destination—Paris.

Chapter 28

The golden lights of the tower shimmered against the deep blue of the night sky as Clara stepped off her train, making her heart swell with excitement. Arriving deep in the night, Clara made her way to her hotel with a fresh eagerness, excited to see the city bloom before her tomorrow in the daylight.

On her first night in Paris, Clara had stayed up deep into the early hours of the morning, meticulously planning her Parisian exploits. Still motivated by the need to make up for lost time, that night, she had booked a reservation at the Hotel Westminster, a classic and elegant establishment located at 13 Rue De La Paix. The hotel was situated perfectly within walking distance of many of the city's iconic landmarks. She had chosen it not for its charm but for the convenience of knowing exactly where she would be staying for the first week. Having forwarded her mail to the General Post Office of Paris, Clara's first stop after checking into her hotel was the post office.

Walking there, Clara thought of all that she'd do in the coming weeks. Obviously, she'd start with the Louvre, where she imagined herself now, working her way towards the famous Venus de Milo statue. She'd dedicate a whole day to the museum, maybe even two. Then she'd go to see the Musée d'Orsay. After that, she'd go to the Tuileries Garden and then the Musée d'Orsay. She was sure the vibrant, dreamy brushstrokes of Monet, the bold compositions of Manet, the delicate dancers of Degas, and the intricate layers of Cezanne and Cassatt would all resonate with her in some way or another. Of course, she'd try and see the Eiffel Tower up close, too, and maybe even try and have a nice dinner near the top.

Then, when she was finally done sightseeing, she'd turn her focus to the Saint-Germain-des-Prés district, where a friend had recommended she stay if she ever found herself looking to live in Paris. If funds got low, she could work in a bookstore or something in the tourism industry. She had been practicing French ever since her face infection got better, anticipating the need for such a skill if she ended up staying in Paris for a substantial amount of time. Her proficiency in the language wasn't as good as she hoped it would be just yet, but she felt it was certainly serviceable. On top of that, she now had years of experience in the tourism industry under her belt from her work on the cruise line.

She was hoping to find a small, quaint studio where she could spend time recharging after work. Eating at cafes in the morning, finding other expatriates to gossip about home, and meeting locals to find all the best restaurants and hidden gems the city had to offer. Maybe she'd even meet the next Monet or Balzac one day; they said Paris was the arts capital of the world. Yes, it all stretched out before her, a dazzling future for the taking.

As she entered the imposing post office, the buzz of daily life in Paris filled her senses. She stood in line, her mind still swirling with the sights she had already taken in. When it was her turn, she stepped up to the counter and spoke to the clerk. "Hi, I'm Clara Schattinger. I've had my mail forwarded here."

The clerk disappeared for a few minutes and returned with a shoebox overflowing with letters. Clara's face lit up with a smile. It was nice to know people were still thinking about her, even after all her time away from home and her old cruise line work.

"Thank you so much. I'll be staying in Paris for several weeks. Could I continue to have my mail forwarded here for the time being?"

The postal clerk nodded and handed her a form. Clara quickly filled out the details: her name, the hotel's address, and her room number, 17. As the clerk wrote her name on a slip of paper and filed it away, Clara felt a small thrill of satisfaction. She was officially set to stay in Paris for a good while now.

A few letters from her parents and one from a friend highlighted the contents of the bundle the postman had handed her. She looked twice over for something from her siblings but found nothing.

"Dad probably mailed it wrong again," Clara thought to herself. How many letters had she gotten in the last few years, months after they were sent because of incorrect postage? "You think they'd learn by now."

Clara swore to herself she would read each and every letter once the day was over and the sun was well under the horizon. Presently, she was too teeming with excitement as it was to waste even a minute more of the day, and she was nearly skipping with joy when she entered the hotel. The front desk clerk called out to her as she made her way to her room. "You- you're Miss Schattinger, aren't you?"

Clara nodded giddily.

"There's a telegram for you."

She took the envelope, her heart a bit heavy with concern. Telegrams were rarely sent for casual reasons, and despite herself, Clara opened it then and there before the front desk clerk.

COME HOME QUICK. MOTHER BROKE HER HIP.

YOUR FATHER.

Chapter 29

Clara took a deep breath as she stepped onto the bustling pier of New York City. The familiar scent of the salty sea air mixed with the distant sound of car horns and chatter from those passing by brought her back to the reality she had been avoiding. Her heart ached, not from the lingering sadness of leaving Paris but also from the uncertainty of what awaited her back home.

The concierge had arranged for a porter to assist her with her luggage. This man swiftly navigated through the throngs of people, leading Clara to the waiting taxi. Clara's mind drifted back to her first visit to New York City as the car drove on when she was young, naïve, and filled with excitement for her sister Joanna's graduation concert. She had fed off the buzz of the city then. Now, it was all too much for her, so much so that she felt nauseous until they finally arrived at Grand Central Station.

The station's iconic clock stood proudly in the center, a testament to time's unrelenting march forward, indifferent to her struggles.

Chapter 29

She was fortunate to have purchased a private compartment for the train ride to Denver, which would take almost two days. Clara looked out the compartment's window once she reached her seat. It was only a matter of minutes before the station began to recede into the rest of the east Clara was leaving behind, and a feeling she could not fully comprehend came over her as she watched the station's iconic clock grow smaller and smaller in the distance, proudly erect and utterly indifferent to her struggles.

Clara then turned her attention to the towering skyscrapers and bustling streets. It was a stark contrast to the tranquil life she had aspired to in Paris. It all seemed so silly to her now that she had believed such a life had really been hers.

Settling into the compartment, she tried to read but couldn't focus on the words. The guilt of not knowing about her mother's condition began to weigh on her too much. Worrying about what to do when she got home ate at Clara even more. She didn't know how to play the role of the supportive daughter or how to be the caring person her mother needed right now. She had never played that role before and warily suspected she wasn't going to be nearly as good at it as she hoped to be.

Reaching for her travel journal, Clara let her emotions spill onto the pages.

"Paris will always be there," she wrote, repeating the words she had told herself so many times. *"I can always go back and try again. But I need to face what's waiting for me in Denver first."*

The rest of the journey was uneventful, though, with each passing hour, Clara thought more and more about the life she wasn't sure she wanted to return to. She felt a deep pang of trepidation as the train finally pulled into the Denver station. She straightened her shoulders and gathered her luggage. There was no turning back now.

The taxi stopped in front of her parents' house. Clara got out as the driver unloaded her trunk and suitcase. As she walked up the front porch steps, she took a big breath and knocked on the door. It was about a full minute before her father finally swung the door open from the inside.

She was shocked by his appearance. How could a person age so quickly in two years? He looked twenty years older. His face was gaunt, and his posture was hunched over. Instead of the strong, tall cattle ranch owner of her childhood

Chapter 29

days. The man in front of her looked exhausted and malnourished, his soiled clothes hanging off his body like a coat hanger.

"Thanks for coming," he said as Clara leaned in to give him a hug. "We need your help."

Clara believed this was the first time in all her life that either of her parents had asked for help. She moved her luggage from the front porch into the front of the living room before following her dad towards the dining room.

Much to her surprise, a twin bed came into Clara's view as she rounded the hall corner. It had been placed in the corner of the room where a China cabinet had once been.

As bad as her father was, Clara's mother was even worse. The woman inside the twin bed had only the slightest resemblance to Clara's mother. The society woman Clara had left behind, with her beautiful skin, hair, and clothes, had since become an unkempt invalid, her eyes sunken and dull. The worn-out little woman looked up and did her best to smile.

"Thank goodness you are home."

The entire downstairs was far messier than Clara had ever seen before. "The live-in housekeeper must be gone," Clara noted to herself as she surveyed the extent of the disarray. The dining room table was stacked with mail and dirty dishes. The kitchen was marked by a dirty floor, sink, and stove. The downstairs bathroom had a filthy sink, shower, and toilet, plus a heap of dirty towels and clothing tucked into the corner. "At least the deep sink and wringer washer look like they still work," Clara thought to herself as she peered out towards the back screened porch.

At last, she moved her luggage from the living room to her bedroom upstairs, except for her trunk. It was the last logical thing she knew to do. After all, where she was to start once she was done unpacking? She took her time putting away each individual piece of clothing in its respective drawers. As she did this, she noticed how little her room had changed since the day she left. A thick layer of dust and a broken dining room chair tucked into the closet were the only changes she could discern before heading back downstairs.

After a dozen or so minutes of deliberation with her dad, the two decided the best place to start was with a trip to the grocery store. The pantry was the one room that wasn't disheveled; it was far too barren for any mess to be made in there. Clara gathered some grocery bags along with her purse while her father wrote a list of things he and Clara's mother needed from the store.

A sudden wave of hunger motivated her. Since there were no other people in the store, Mr. Randall helped her gather her cleaning supplies and produce. She would go next door to the meat market for the remaining items.

The monotony of finding item after item at the grocery store did well to calm Clara's nerves, and she thought of herself as a bit dramatic for having stressed out so much upon returning home. Then she came in through the front door, and the stale bleakness of the house's air sent her spiraling all over again.

"You two really need to get some light in here," Clara complained as she opened curtain after curtain. "There, that's better," she said triumphantly as she opened the final curtain. But the house was as dull and depressing as ever, as though the dreariness of the house transcended lighting or cleanliness.

Back home, she retrieved her mother's largest pot, scrubbed it, and started cooking the whole chicken while she began cleaning the kitchen. She was pleased that Mr. Randall put a pair of rubber gloves into her bag. For the remainder of the day, she filled the bucket with hot, soapy water several times. Clara cleaned the kitchen counter and a set of pots and pans. She had bought ingredients for chicken noodle soup, and after an hour of cleaning she was finally able to start her work on the meal.

Clara began chopping the vegetables for the soup as the chicken cooked. She called her Dad in to talk as she did so.

"How has she gotten this bad?" Clara asked in a hushed voice once he was in the room. "You said she broke her hip over the telegram, but she looks like someone who only has a few more months to live right now."

Clara's father sighed heavily and began to explain how it had all gone so wrong.

"She sustained a minor hip fracture after falling in the kitchen. After a few days at Denver General, the doctors determined that she was a high risk for surgery because of her heart condition. They sent her home and encouraged her to use a walker around the house until her hip healed and she was steady on her feet. But you know your mother," he said with another sigh.

"She thinks of herself as a society woman, and she wouldn't dare be seen in public with a walker. She hasn't gotten out of bed since the day we came back from the hospital."

"Have you been taking care of her since then?"

Her father gave a small nod.

"No wonder he looks so exhausted," Clara thought to herself. "She's probably been working him to the bone."

"Here," her father said, interrupting her thoughts. "Let me finish the cooking. You go give your mother a bath. She's been nagging me to give her one all day, but it's starting to get hard for me. My knees don't bend the same as they did back on the ranch."

Clara had never given any person a bed bath. Her father explained the fundamentals of the process to her as he finished cutting the vegetables, then shooed Clara off after a small wail came from the dining room bed. She gathered the single clean towel from the clothesline before making her way to her mother.

"Clara!" she heard her mother calling from the other room. Clara hurriedly filled a dishpan with warm water and grabbed a bar of soap out of the clean bathroom.

She talked to her mother every step of the bath. Clara noticed that her mother's left buttock was developing an ulcer, probably due to the bedpan. She packed the wound with cream and dry gauze but had no idea if it would help or hurt. She washed her back and legs, then between her legs. Her skin was fragile and thin. Clara rubbed lotion off her hands and massaged her mother's arms, legs, hands, and feet. She changed the water, washed her mother's face, and rubbed the damp washcloth on her mother's hair.

Her mother talked a bit during her bath, but it was all drama and rumors about families Clara had long forgotten existed.

"Thank you," she said as Clara finished her bath. "I haven't been this clean and relaxed in months."

Clara had her mother roll from side to side so she could put the less dirty sheets on the mattress, then she changed the top sheet and pillowcase. At the end, Clara gathered the wet towels and sheets and again started another load of laundry. To finish off her mother's bath, Clara combed her hair and braided it. From the kitchen Clara's father announced the soup was going well and would be ready for dinner. She would have to add the noodles later.

Once the chicken noodle soup was done, Clara took her cleaning supplies upstairs to her bathroom. There were no towels in the room. Clara speculated there likely hadn't been a towel in it in years.

Before she started scrubbing, she removed the lace curtains and dingy green cotton rug. Then she scrubbed to remove the grime and rust in the sink, tub, and toilet before attempting to clean the floor, windowsill, and mirror. The pipes under the sink needed replacement, but not today. Before going back downstairs, she removed the sheets and blankets on her bed. Thank goodness the mattress had a protective cover. She sprayed disinfectant on the protective cover and wiped it dry. That at least made her bedroom smell fresh.

Following a quick break, she started again with another load of laundry, which she hung out to dry before finishing dinner. In the end, about eight hours of work put the smallest of dents into the house. Still, it was a dent. She tried to pride herself on this.

After drinking a few glasses of water, she put a box of dry noodles in the broth. She then set the table for three people, relieved her father of his cooking duties, and asked her mother if she would like to try to walk to the table.

Her mother glared at her.

"If I wanted to get out of bed, I would have gotten out of bed when you were trying to change the sheets. I need my food on a tray in bed."

Thus, Clara realized what kind of person her mother had become.

She thought to herself, "I will take care of her now, for as long as she lives, like she cared for me as a child. I might have to."

A timer went off, notifying Clara that the soup was done. Clara removed the place setting and arranged a tray with a small bowl of soup, several crackers, and a cup of water. She placed it on the over-the-bed-side table. Her mother took one glance at it and said, "I need hot tea for lunch. Not water."

Clara sighed.

"I'll make your tea, but please try to eat the soup while it's still hot."

"I will wait for the tea."

Clara served her father a large bowl of soup, a small sandwich, and a glass of water. By the time the water boiled for her mother's tea, he had devoured his lunch.

He said, "That soup was delicious. Is there enough for a second helping?"

Until today, Clara had been much more accustomed to being served rather than serving meals.

The hot tea was served along with another bowl of soup for her father. She collected the dishes and finally had time to eat a bowl of soup herself. Clara realized how hungry she was after the first couple of bites. It made sense; she had been too busy to eat any breakfast, and now it was almost past lunchtime as well. After two bowls of chicken noodle soup, she made herself a sandwich as well.

"This is only the first day, and I am drowning in work and demands." She wanted to shout this to someone, but who? Steve? There was no one there for her anymore like that. Everyone in the house was everyone she wanted to complain about.

By the time she cleaned the dishes, it was time to think about cooking dinner. All Clara wanted to do was take a nap.

The next day was much like that one as was the next and the one after that. Some days and nights went by quickly, and others dragged on for many hours. Every day included cleaning, cooking, and caring for her parents. Her only breaks were her walks to and from the grocery and meat market each day.

The more Clara tried to adjust to being a full-time caregiver, the more she resented it. None of her three siblings had made any contact with her parents or her in the next two weeks, even though they all three lived in the Denver area. One day she decided finally to try and call each one from a phone booth at the end of the block. They never answered.

Chapter 30

Clara began setting her alarm clock an hour earlier than usual, a week or so after moving in. She found that this was the only way she could have some quiet time to herself before the day's tasks inevitably forced her downstairs. In the still darkness of her room, she would sit with her hands on her knees, trying to think about anything else besides the day's chores that awaited her. This most often meant thinking about all the places she'd rather be in that house, about all the things she'd rather be doing than those chores that awaited her with the rising of the sun. Then her room would light up, always too soon, Clara felt, and her day would begin again.

Many days the only thing that would bring Clara some semblance of happiness was the condition of the house. Over the few months she'd been home, Clara had managed to clean what felt like every inch of the entire house. She scrubbed and rinsed every rug in the house with hose water.

Her father did his best to help Clara whenever he could. Soon after she arrived, he agreed to have a telephone installed, bought her a new vacuum cleaner, and fixed the wringer washing machine when it broke. But he could hardly help her with anything that required physical exertion. He was far too frail for any of that now. This didn't keep him from volunteering to help Clara whenever she began cleaning, however, and in time Clara began giving him inane tasks whose sole purpose was to keep her father from taxing his body too much.

As for her mother, Clara eventually got her to consent to Clara's transferring her from the bed to the commode and sometimes even into an armed chair. There, she would sit long enough for Clara to change the bed linen and freshen up her pillows and blankets.

Clara often mentioned the possibility of buying a wheelchair for her mother, much to her mother's irritation. But Clara did not give up on the idea, which often seemed like her only real way of escape. Clara believed that, with a wheelchair, there was a chance of jump-starting her mother's path to recovery. She was almost sure that if her mother would only go out into society once in the chair, she may remember everything she was missing out on by staying cooped up in this house. Then, she might finally start doing the exercises the doctors recommended, making efforts to groom herself and caring about her health again. If she could only get her mother in the wheelchair, a path might open where Clara's father would be able to care for her on his own.

"It would be so nice to push you out onto the front porch for a little fresh air," Clara would say to her mother whenever the idea came up.

"The pain's too bad for that," her mother would always say without fail, "and I'd rather be dead than seen like that, anyway."

The conviction in her mother's voice often made Clara believe she'd see her mother in a coffin before a wheelchair. What would become of herself, then? Just getting out of this house seemed like a possibility that could be years in the making, much less a return to her travels abroad. Always, she shooed the idea away as soon as it came to her, and always it came back with an even greater vengeance than before.

It took about two weeks for Clara to notice that her father was walking slower, holding his side as he did so. One day, when he nearly fell while holding his right side, Clara decided it was finally time to bring the matter up with him.

"Are you alright?" she said as she helped him back up.

"Oh, I'm fine. Just a little pain in my abdomen. Nothing serious."

"Should I schedule an appointment with Dr. Steiner?"

Her father took a moment to respond, righting himself before he did so.

"Only if you really want to," her father said, but Clara could tell from his face that this idea brought some relief to her father. She could tell from his exasperated effort to smile that he must have been in serious pain. She called Dr. Steiner later that afternoon.

The day of the appointment was a dreary, rainy one. Clara and her father shuffled into the office in cold and soggy clothes. Then, for about fifteen minutes, she was forced to watch her father shiver uncontrollably as they sat in the waiting lobby. The only available chairs were below an A/C vent, which blew down on them hard for what felt like hours, and her father refused to move anywhere else. The pain of walking was that bad now. Finally, her father's name was called.

"Do you want me to be with you when the doctor does his tests?" Clara asked as her father slowly got up.

Her father nodded silently. He had grown to trust Clara a great deal in the passing months.

After waiting alone together in their assigned room for a few minutes, a tall, good-looking man in a white coat came in and greeted Clara and her father. Dr. Steiner had been her father's doctor ever since they'd come to Denver, and so it wasn't until after a handful of friends and family members were talked about did the doctor finally asked questions about Clara's father himself and the problems he was having.

It took a while for her father to list them all. Clara soon realized he'd been having more trouble than she initially thought. Meanwhile, Dr. Steiner listened to Henry's symptoms with professional patience and interest. Clara added a few more details once her father finished. Dr. Steiner nodded and said he'd like to run a few tests on Mr. Schattinger if that was alright with the two of them.

A small sample of blood and an X-ray were taken that day. Two weeks later, a letter came in the mail letting Clara know her father was anemic.

"So that's why he's always looking so pale," Clara thought as she read the results. But this was almost a relief. She knew anemia could be cured in most cases.

A month later, Clara got a call from Dr. Steiner. He needed to see her father at once regarding a large tumor they'd found in his abdomen.

"This tumor is eight centimeters big," Dr. Steiner told Clara over the phone.

"And that's pretty big?"

"Yes, for an abdomen tumor, it's certainly quite large. The tests also give us reason to believe it's malignant. We think it's going to spread to other organs soon if it has not already done so."

"So, we operate, right?" Clara interjected.

"Usually, yes. But with your father, well… it's my opinion that he is too frail to endure such an operation. Besides, while we can't say this for certain yet, I'm willing to bet his cancer has already metastasized. That would make operating totally out of the question in his case."

"Then what can we do?" Clara said. Tears were starting to come. Despite herself, she felt angry with Dr. Steiner. It was difficult to remember that he was only the diagnostician of all this, not the cause.

"You're welcome to get a consultation somewhere else. I can refer you to other doctors if you'd like. But right now, all I can do is write up a prescription for your father to get some pain medication. Miss Schattinger, I want you to know that I am very, truly sorry for your father. I can only imagine what-"

"How much longer does he have to live?" Clara interrupted. She wanted this conversation to end as soon as possible, and this was the single piece of information she still needed. The line was silent for long enough that Clara began to worry that the call had been disconnected. It was as Clara thought to check the machine that she heard Dr. Steiner's voice again.

"I would estimate he has about 2-3 months to live."

Clara did not hang up then, as she had planned. Instead, she listened to Dr. Steiner prattle about how Clara could rent a hospital bed from him if she wanted, how she could hire a nurse to come and work at her house a few hours each day, and how she would have to pick up the prescription for her father's pain medication. In the end, it was Dr. Steiner who hung up on Clara. She didn't even know that the conversation was over until the tone began buzzing in her ear.

"Who was that?" Her mother groaned from the other room. "How many times have I told you not to use your phone to call up your friends? We don't have that kind of money. But no, you never listen to me, do you?"

All Clara wanted to do was go upstairs and cry without restraint then, but instead, she found herself habitually asking whether her mother needed anything. Soon, she was changing her mother's diaper, cleaning up her bed, and heating up her soup lunch, all the while fighting off tears.

Clara waited until her mother was comfortable, and then she pulled a chair over to the side of her mother's bed.

"That wasn't a call with a friend," Clara began.

"Then a boyfriend? That would be just like you, to get into romantics now when it does nobody no good. You don't even have the look for that stuff anymore. If you'd only married John

Chapter 30

Aberdeen or Lucas Robertson, I bet we wouldn't have been in this mess."

"It wasn't a boy, either, Mom," Clara said. "It was Dr. Steiner."

"Not that quack! I can't believe you two went to see him. What'd he call you for, then? To tell you that Dad needs wrist or knee surgery. He did, didn't he? I can see it on your face. You know, sometimes you seem to forget it, but your father is still that strong man who managed a 640-acre ranch and all its staff, too. Don't believe a word of whatever that quack says. Your father's just getting old. I don't need a doctorate to tell you that."

"He has cancer, Mom," Clara said, fully expecting to be interrupted by her mother before she could continue. But her mother only looked at her blankly, as though she wasn't even there.

"It's in his abdomen. A tumor is eight centimeters big, I think Dr. Steiner said. They saw it on his X-rays. They say we shouldn't operate either. He explained why, but I forgot already. I'm sorry."

"Anything else?" her mother said.

"Dr. Steiner wrote a prescription for Dad to get a bottle of pain pills. I'm going to pick it up tomorrow."

"Did they say anything about timelines?"

Clara hesitated for a moment.

"No, nothing," she answered. "I want to tell his brother, Peter, and Mary, Joanna and George, my siblings. Do you have a problem with me using the phone for that?" Clara added testily.

"If you think it's that serious, fine. But I do not want any of them to come and go in and out of the house. I already have enough headaches from you moving stuff around and taking phone calls and dragging your feet on the carpet as it is."

"Dr. Steiner gave me some information about the Visiting Nurses Association. I think I'm going to call them, too, to see how much it would cost for a nurse to start coming over here to help me."

"No!" Her mother sat up fully in bed so that Clara thought for a moment she was going to pop right out of it and stand up like nothing had ever happened, if only so that she could come over there and smack Clara herself. "No stranger is coming into my house. Especially not a nurse. I've heard stories about them stealing jewelry."

"Oh yes, all the jewelry you go out wearing every day down at the yacht club. Wouldn't want them taking that! God forbid your necklaces and bracelets and rings do not rack up more dust, you damn invalid!"

Clara had been saving up that word for a while now. Invalid.

It had had its intended effects: Clara's mother looked redder in the face than Clara could ever remember before. She was so mad that she had begun choking on her words. Clara slammed the door behind her before her mother could get a full sentence out, heading straight to the phone after she did so, meaning to call up Dr. Steiner again. However, to her surprise, beside the phone was her notepad, and on the front page of that notepad were ten digits labeled 'Nursing Association.' She must have jotted down unknowingly while in her trance. Clara dialed the number.

The hospital bed came a week later. Clara was on the verge of tears as the two delivery men helped install it on the other side of the dining room. She had such great respect for her father, and now to see where he'd soon become an invalid like her mother, where he may very well die in a matter of weeks, was too much for her. She went upstairs before they were finished.

A nap numbed some of Clara's agony that day, which came back only at half-strength when she saw the bed again in the dining room. It was now fully installed and ready for her father. The delivery men had let themselves out.

Clara cleaned the kitchen and started to give her mother a short bed bath with a clean nightgown in hopes of her sleeping all night. After that, she helped her father get into his clean pajamas. Clara's assistant, a nurse named Linda, helped Clara's father into the bed. As a professional, she knew how to help him get comfortable in the hospital bed within a few minutes.

"You know, Clara, this bed is more comfortable than I expected," her father said as he settled in. His tone was a little sing-songy now from the pain medication. If things had been different, Clara might have asked Dr. Steiner if this meant her father was taking too much of the medication and whether they should worry that he might become addicted in time. As it was, she nearly hoped her father was stoned. If it made him happier, well, that was all she could ask for.

Chapter 30

"Thanks again for all this. I hope that I can get out of it to help your mom during the night."

"Why are you thanking Clara? Linda was the one that helped you in bed. Thank her!"

"Oh, yes, thank you, Linda," Clara's father said guiltily.

"Don't worry about it, Mr. Schattinger," Linda said.

"Oh, you're too humble, Linda! Clara could never have done what you did there. She might have killed him if she were the one helping him into the bed."

"Please, Mrs. Schattinger, Clara does her best."

"Her best is shit."

Clara sighed and left the room to grab her father's pain medication. He'd be needing more soon. Linda gave her an empathizing smile as she left, but Clara could not bring herself to return it.

Despite her mother's qualms, Clara had hired a nurse over the phone the very day she and her mother had had their fight. The next day, Linda came.

Initially, Clara's mother was as hostile to Linda as imaginable. But it only took a couple of days for her mother to start warming up to Linda, and soon, the two began talking for hours on end while Linda helped Clara's father with his own needs. At first, Clara thought this was a good thing. In time, she realized her mother's aim.

"So, you have two sons? I'm sure they're adorable. You know, Clara never married. I didn't even try to. Yes, she had her pick of men at one time, believe it or not. And now look at her. She's certainly not the proud mother of two sons, that's for sure."

In this way, Linda soon became everything that Clara was not for her mother, and this one fact dominated the conversation every time Linda was around. For her part, Linda was sweet and defended Clara, but this only gave her mother more opportunities to tear her daughter down. When she returned downstairs with the medication, Clara was moderately surprised that her mother didn't make a comment on how Linda would've gotten the medication faster.

"I'm going to start sleeping on the couch for a few nights," Clara said as she handed her father his two pills. "That way, I can help you both in case something happens in the night."

Her father threw the pill into his mouth like a piece of candy, downing it without water or anything else.

"Linda recommended this since I might not be able to hear you if I am upstairs."

"I'm actually thinking of leaving now if that's alright with you," Linda said. Clara looked at the clock.

"It's only quarter past nine."

"Mike has soccer practice tonight, and I need to pick him up. My husband's sick. You don't mind, do you?"

"Of course, she doesn't mind!" Clara's mother interjected loudly. "Clara can be tough, but she'd never keep a mother away from her sons. Now you go, Linda, and you tell Mikey we all said hi!"

And so, Linda left an hour and forty-five minutes early.

"Mom, we pay Linda to be here from three to eleven each day. You can't just let her leave like that."

"You heard her, her son was going to be left all alone at the fields if she didn't go get him! Is that what you wanted?"

"No, but – I at least wanted to see if we wouldn't have to pay her for the extra hour and forty-five minutes she's leaving us for."

"You wouldn't dare! Linda needs that money to support her boys!"

Clara's mother talked of Linda's sons with as much pride as a grandmother despite the fact neither of the two had ever met her. They likely didn't even know she existed.

"But–" Clara began but stopped herself short. She was too tired to be arguing with her mother, now or anytime else it felt like. Her father's needs had increased rapidly in the passing weeks, so Clara had to be ready virtually every hour of the day. Linda was gone in case he needed help with whichever new problem the day brought on.

Clara had begun sleeping during the day now so that Linda could care for the two while she was asleep. She had woken up an hour ago and had been hoping to get an extra hour of sleep before Linda left. "So much for that," Clara thought as she laid back down on the sofa, face first into the cushions. She lay there for all of two minutes before her mother began calling for food.

Clara developed a routine of walking to the grocery store every other day, doing laundry every day, and managing the Schattingers' small vegetable garden whenever she had the chance. From eleven to one was her time away from her parents' growing needs. She spent this time doing chores as well as leisurely activities. On Mondays, she walked to the Denver Public Library to return books and check out new ones. This was one of the few activities which consistently brought her joy now. Some nights, she read poetry to her father, who especially appreciated whatever Clara could find of Walt Whitman. Her mother's interest in the poems only went so far as criticizing them or telling Clara to read them less loudly.

About a month after her father's diagnosis, Clara saw a few pieces of mail with her name on it among the rest of the bills and junk mail. A closer look showed these letters had been forwarded from the Paris hotel where she had left her address. One letter from Hazel had been forwarded twice, as well as a surprising postcard from Steve.

Hi Clara, I hope that you are doing well in Denver. Thinking of you, Steve.

She did not recall ever mentioning to Steve that she would be returning to Denver. Had he been tracking her whereabouts through his FBI position? The thought gave her a chill.

"It doesn't matter," Clara told herself as she opened the envelope containing Hazel's letter, "I don't have time to be worrying about him, anyway."

Hazel's letter focused on cruise gossip, much of which centered on those Guest Ambassadors the two had known from their training together. But Clara could hardly find it in her to finish reading the letter; these people were a part of the life she had left behind, on some boat thousands of miles away from her now. Seeing their names in the letter felt very much like reading a novel whose characters she could barely remember, much less care about.

She then turned her attention to the mail addressed to her parents. Bills and a couple of jargon-filled letters from lawyers. Clara's father was coherent enough to take Dr. Steiner's advice to organize his money and legal issues. As always, she looked twice over through the mail for any other letters from her siblings. As always, no mail ever came.

Chapter 31

Clara accompanied her father to Dr. Steiner's office on Monday. Though Henry was feeling slightly better, Clara had made her father agree to go to the doctor's office at least once a month following his diagnosis. The time had come for January's appointment, and so the two were now sitting in their assigned room silently, waiting for Dr. Steiner. Clara's father read and reread one of the posters on the wall. Clara carefully watched the clock tick on. To the relief of both, a knock on the other side of the door came a few minutes after they sat down.

"Hello, Mr. and Miss Schattinger," Dr. Steiner said as he entered the exam room.

"Hello, Dr. Steiner," said Clara's father, with all the calmness of a man in for nothing more than a simple check-up.

"How are you, Henry?"

"Pretty good, I'd say," Clara's father said. It was only when Clara loudly cleared her throat that

Mr. Schattinger lifted his chin up a bit and added to his response, in a much more serious tone,

"Well, not all too good, that is. I am getting weaker, but the pain is slightly less."

"Thanks for the updates, Henry. What you're describing is what we would expect from someone in your situation. As the tumor grows, it will keep using up more and more of your energy. Conversely, as the nerves dissolve, the pain diminishes. It's a bit of a double-edged sword, isn't it?"

"Sounds like it," said Clara's father with a laugh. Clara let a slight sigh slip out, then felt it was her time to join the conversation.

"What's his timeline looking like?" asked Clara.

"What do you mean by that, exactly, Miss Schattinger?"

"Please, doctor. We can handle a blunt answer. Right, Dad?"

Clara's father nodded and gave a small, meek smile.

"Well, as of right now, the cancer is spreading throughout your father's – Henry's – body. Once the cancer invades the bones, his pain will begin increasing again, worse than before. Like I said during your last visit, we can implement some new medication when this happens. Liquid morphine, probably, so he should never be in any severe pain. No need to worry about that end stage."

"But how much longer do I have to live, Dr. Steiner?" Clara's father intervened, reading the look on his daughter's face.

"I cannot predict a date like that. In your situation, some patients live for weeks, others for months, some for years. But, as I suggested previously, I do highly recommend getting your legal affairs sorted out as quickly as possible."

The talk then transitioned to that of mutual friends between Dr. Steiner and Mr. Schattinger so that the two men talked of the dying man's cancer for five minutes and a friend's new boat for twenty-five minutes. Clara watched the clock tick on through it all.

Father and daughter went out to eat following the appointment, as had been planned the previous day.

"Clara," her father began once the waiter had taken their orders, "I want all our money to go to you."

"Dad, you know you can't do something like…"

"Let me finish, please," he said, interrupting his daughter with a severity of tone she no longer thought possible in him. She nodded silently.

"You have taken care of both your mother and me ever since you came back," he continued. "And you have done an excellent job, too. You are a responsible person through and through. I'd like to think you've got a little of that from me."

The meek smile came over his face again, then faded almost instantaneously.

"As for your three siblings, they have not as much as stopped by to say hello. I am so embarrassed by your siblings, to the point that I refuse to even speak their names anymore. George, Mary, and Joanna – they deserve nothing from your mother and me. But for you, well, I only wish there were a better way to pay you back for our interrupting your life. If only we could give you back all the time you spent with us on top of the money."

Chapter 31

"Thanks, Dad. That really is kind of you and mother, though I wish you'd at least give the others something, even if it is only a small amount."

Mr. Schattinger shook his head solemnly at this suggestion.

"Nothing."

"Well, we can always talk about that another time. Right now, I have a few questions for you."

"Legal questions?" her father said.

"Of course. You heard the doctor."

"Go ahead."

"First," Clara began, pulling a pen and a notebook from her purse, from which she read aloud, "who is your attorney?"

"Mr. Bailey. He works downtown."

"Do you know his number?" Clara read the next question from the notebook while writing down the answer to the last.

"Not by heart, but it should be on the tablet next to my bed.

Does he have a copy of your will?"

"I hope so," chuckled Mr. Schattinger. "He was the one who drafted it."

"And did he do Mother's will, too?"

Her father nodded.

"Your mother's will is the same as mine."

"Do you still own the ranch in South Park?"

"In a way. Your uncle Peter bought the ranch from us when we moved to Denver. But it's his son, your cousin, Walter, who runs the ranch now."

"But what do you mean when you say you still own it 'in a way'?"

"Your mother and I still have partial ownership of it. I only agreed to sell it to Peter because he let me keep a minority stake in it. Each winter, Walter comes down to Denver to give me my share of the profits or, more recently, to explain why there were no profits that year. Still, even if it's not the gold mine it used to be, both Peter and I would like the ranch to stay with the family. Mr. Bailey knows how to contact Peter and Walter if you need."

"But I don't know anything about running the ranch," said Clara.

"You can talk to Peter about that after I pass away, or even before then if you really want. He knows the details, so he can help you with the arrangements."

Having crossed off the final question on her list, Clara let out a sigh of relief.

"Thanks, Dad. That helps a lot."

"You are most welcome, Clara."

Their food came shortly after this final exchange, and it was in a much less tense silence than before that the two ate their meal.

The restaurant was in the opposite direction of their home, so Clara decided it best to hail a taxi. The ride cut what would have been an hour's walk into a five-minute ride. Once they arrived, the taxi driver helped Clara get her father out of the backseat and into the house.

"Where have you been for so long?" a voice called from the kitchen as soon as the door opened. "I'm starving. Haven't eaten anything all day!"

"Yes, Mother, I will get you your lunch," Clara said as she tipped the taxi driver extra and closed the front door. "I told the visiting nurse to come later since Dad had his appointment. Does soup work?"

"No, that will take too long. Make me a cheese sandwich."

Henry managed to crawl into bed while Clara made the requested cheese sandwich.

Later that afternoon, while both her parents were conveniently napping, Clara decided to search for her father's tablet for the phone number of Mr. Bailey, the attorney. She found it easily, then dialed the number into the home phone. The dial buzzed in Clara's ear for no longer than a moment before a woman's voice came through the other side.

"Hello, this is Bailey and Shanker Law Firm. How may I help you?"

"Hello, this is Clara Schattinger. My father is Henry Schattinger. I would like to talk to Mr. Bailey, please."

The other side of the line was silent for a few moments.

"Lucky you, Mr. Bailey just got out of a two-hour meeting with a client. I'm putting you through to his office now. Have a nice day!"

Chapter 31

The noise of the dial returned momentarily, then was interrupted by the deep voice of a man introducing himself as Mr. Bailey.

"Hello, Mr. Bailey. I don't think we've met, but I'm the daughter of one of your clients, Harry Schattinger."

"Clara! No, we haven't met, but your father talks about you so much I feel as though we almost have!" The deep voice let out a deeper chuckle. "What can I do for you? Is this about your father's cancer diagnosis?"

"He told you about it, then?"

"Yes, the other week, we talked about it over the phone."

"I am glad to hear that," Clara said. "Unfortunately, my father's condition has been getting worse and worse lately."

"So, you're calling me to discuss his will, I imagine?"

"Exactly. I was hoping you could tell me what I need to do at this point to be prepared."

"Clara, you can rest assured that your parents have taken care of every detail of their wills. A few months ago, you were made the sole heir to their inheritance. As your siblings are disadvantaged by this change, they might try to dispute the will, saying your father wasn't in full possession of his mental faculties when making this alteration. I'd go as far as to say they are likely to attempt that move."

"Should I start preparing for a court case or a lawsuit, then?" Clara said in approbation.

"Oh no, no. I'm sorry to have startled you like that. Please don't worry about this. The only strain such a move would cause would be an emotional one. Anticipating this move, I expressly sent for two notaries to be present in the room when these alterations were made, one of whom certified your father as being of sound mind. What I should've said, then, was that your sibling may try to dispute your parents' wills, but they will not win in court. Now then, do you have any other questions?"

"Yes, do you know the name of my parents' estate banker?"

"Yes, his name is Donald Williams. We have been friends for many years. He works at the Bank of Colorado in the estate department. I have kept him up to date on these recent developments after receiving your father's permission. Donald and your parents have been friends since they moved from South Park. If you have a pencil, I will give you his telephone number."

"No need. My father has his number next to your number, but he forgot to include his name, so thank you for that."

The lawyer asked Clara if she had any more questions. When Clara said she did not, he extended her an invitation to his office whenever he might be of use to her and rang off.

Hours turned into days, days into weeks. Henry continually grew weaker after the appointment and soon needed the liquid morphine prescribed to ease the now very prominent pain. Clara's appreciation for the visiting nurses also grew, as their visits remained the sole reason Clara was able to get enough sleep to cope with each day. When the date of his February appointment came, Henry was too weak to go in.

One morning, the night nurse approached Clara with a grave look on her face. Clara feared for a moment she was about to declare her resignation.

"Your father had a difficult time last night," was all she said. Clara almost let out a sigh of relief.

"He has difficult nights every night now."

The nurse shook her head vehemently.

"Not like last night. He was hallucinating. Please, Miss Schattinger, I know about these things. I have seen them in many other patients."

"But he's not hallucinating now, is he?" Clara asked.

"No, he has not been responsive this morning except for moaning in pain."

"So then, you're thinking…"

"That he does not have many days left to live, yes."

Clara tried to respond and found she could not. It seemed the nurse was also familiar with such reactions to this news, as she put a caressing arm and Clara's shoulder and said in as reassuring a voice as she could muster,

"Would you like me to stay a little longer so you can get dressed and have breakfast before you take over his care?"

Chapter 31

"Oh, yes, you are so kind to offer to stay. It won't be for long, I promise. I'll get dressed now and will be right back. Promise."

As Clara walked into her bedroom, she struggled not to burst into tears. She had known this day was coming for a long time now, and yet the news still struck her with all the force of Dr. Steiner's first diagnosis. However, she managed to get dressed and let the nurse leave before the hour was up. While her father slept, she made breakfast for her mother and coffee for herself.

"Father had a restless night," Clara told her mother as the oatmeal cooked in the other room. "The nurse kept him comfortable, but she said that he was not himself. She does not think he will live more than a few days."

"I know, I know. I heard him last night. He was loud enough to wake me up a handful of times, not to mention the nurse walking around his bed all night. Have you made my breakfast yet? Poor sleep makes me even hungrier than usual, I think."

"Yes, I made your usual breakfast of oatmeal and toast. Is that okay?"

"It will have to be ok if that's what you made," Clara's mother said with a grimace.

As Clara returned to the kitchen, she promised herself that she would never become a bitter old woman like her mother.

"I'd rather die than that," she inwardly vowed to herself.

After making a second cup of coffee, Clara returned to serve her mother's breakfast. On the way to her father's bed, she put some classical music on the radio. While he slept, Clara watched the snow fall out of the living room window. Tears intermittently ran down her cheeks.

Clara wasted no time—she called the nursing agency and requested round-the-clock care for her mother. For the next few days, her sole focus would be her father. Let the nurses deal with her mother's insatiable need for attention.

Sleep didn't matter. Hunger didn't register. The only thing that existed was the fragile rise and fall of her father's chest. She clung to his hand, her mind unraveling a flood of memories—his unwavering support, the letters he sent as she wandered the world, the quiet pride in his eyes when she chased her dreams. Unlike her mother's sporadic, indifferent notes, his letters were lifelines. He had planned everything—even his will—ensuring that she, his beloved daughter, would inherit everything. But what was an estate without him? The thought of a world where he wasn't her anchor, where she drifted alone in a city that suddenly felt foreign, was unbearable.

She willed time to slow, but it was relentless. The hours bled into each other. Days passed unnoticed. The sun rose and fell, but she remained—watching, waiting. And then, it happened.

The moment she dreaded came in silence. One last breath, then stillness. She didn't move. She didn't cry. She simply stayed, gripping his hand as if she could tether his spirit a moment longer. The nurse made the call. The coroner arrived at daybreak. At some point, someone must have told her mother, but Clara had no recollection of it.

At forty-four years old, she never needed her father's wisdom more. But now, his voice was only an echo in her heart, and she was left to navigate the world without him.

Henry Schattinger passed away peacefully early on February 23, 1932. He was buried at Crown Hill Cemetery in Denver, Colorado. Citing pain of her own, Clara's mother chose not to attend.

There was a simple service at the cemetery chapel followed by the burial. Clara's siblings, George, Mary, and Joanna, attended the service only, throughout which none of the four spoke to each other. A few days later Clara got a phone call from Mr. Bailey, letting her know that, as he had predicted, each of her siblings had begun legal procedures to contest the will. But their efforts were in vain, and by the end of the week Mr. Bailey called Clara again, this time to let her know he'd received a motion from the judge to dismiss the case. It was to be Clara's last interaction with her family for over a decade.

Clara continued to be the primary caregiver for her mother for the next 13 years after her father's death. Her mother passed away on November 9, 1945, at the age of 88 years old. Clara was 58 by then, nearly twice the age she had been when she first left Colorado for Hawaii.

P.S.

About the author

Kay Perrin, PhD: A Life of Dedication, Adventure, and Lifelong Learning

Born and raised in Denver, Colorado, Kay Perrin's life has been marked by her academic achievements, professional success, and global adventures. After graduating with her nursing degree, Kay went on to work as a full-time nurse. However, after over a decade in this field, she repivoted her life in a new direction, enrolling at the University of South Florida (USF) in her 40's. There she earned her Master's and PhD in Public Health, then continued on at USF as a faculty member for 26 years, where she rose to the position of Associate Dean of Public Health.

While employed at USF, Kay worked to further public health education at a local and international level. Her work abroad most notably included a six-month trip to Pune, India, where she taught nursing and supervised student rotations as a Fulbright Scholar. By the time of her retirement, Kay had authored five public health textbooks and helped create Florida's first undergraduate Public Health degree at USF.

Following her retirement, Kay has begun channeling her energy and creativity into new outlets. She adores spending time with her two sons, Scott and Andrew, as well as her five grandchildren and two dogs. In her free time, Kay takes comedy classes and has begun writing historical fiction, with her debut novel "The Spinster That I Once Knew" representing what she hopes will be the first of many works.

Discussion Questions

1. If you were to write your autobiography, at what point in your life would you begin, and why?
2. What chapter of your life story would you consider the most meaningful or exciting to write about?
3. If you had a grocery store within walking distance of your home, would you visit daily for fresh food, or would you prefer to stock up less frequently?
4. Why do you think Clara only shared stories about the captain, his yacht, and his seven children with the family?
5. What might be the deeper reason behind Clara's reluctance to unpack her trunk?
6. Knowing she was a millionaire after her parents' passing, why do you think Clara chose to live as a recluse without modern conveniences like a phone or refrigerator?
7. Do you believe Kay's parents were entitled to receive any portion of Clara's estate? Why or why not?

8. What significance might there be in Clara frequently mentioning the businessmen living upstairs?
9. Why did Clara insist that Kay sit on the trunk during each visit and never allow her to explore other parts of the house?
10. If Clara was your sibling, how would you respond to her phone calls? Would you maintain a close relationship with her?
11. Was Clara's decision to leave the nursing home and return home the right choice? Why or why not?
12. Do you believe Clara was truly depressed, or was she simply living life on her own terms, even if it was unconventional?
13. How do you interpret Clara's attachment to her trunk? Do you think it symbolizes something deeper about her past or personality?
14. What role do you think isolation played in shaping Clara's later years? Do you view her solitude as empowering or tragic?
15. If you could ask Clara one question about her life, what would it be?